MARY ANN SPENCER PULASKI

understanding
PIAGET

an introduction to children's cognitive development

HARPER & ROW, PUBLISHERS

NEW YORK, EVANSTON, SAN FRANCISCO, LONDON

1817

By the same author

Learning to Use Our Language

Grateful acknowledgment is given to the following:

International Universities Press, Inc., and Delachaux & Niestle, Neuchâtel, Switzerland, for *The Origins of Intelligence in Children*, by Jean Piaget.

Longman Group Limited and The Viking Press, Inc., for *Science of Education and the Psychology of the Child*, by Jean Piaget. Translated by Derek Coltman. Copyright © 1969 by Editions Denoel, Paris. English translation copyright © 1970 by Grossman Publishers, Inc. Reprinted by permission of Grossman Publishers.

Routledge & Kegan Paul Ltd. and Humanities Press Inc. for *The Child's Conception of the World* and *The Child's Conception of Number*, by Jean Piaget.

Routledge & Kegan Paul Ltd. and Basic Books, Inc., Publishers, for *The Growth of Logical Thinking from Childhood to Adolescence*, by Bärbel Inhelder and Jean Piaget. Translated by Anne Parsons and Stanley Milgram. Basic Books, Inc., Publishers, New York, 1958.

Routledge & Kegan Paul Ltd. and Basic Books, Inc., Publishers, for *The Child's Conception of Time*, by Jean Piaget. Translated by A. J. Pomerans. English translation copyright © 1969 by Routledge & Kegan Paul Ltd. and Basic Books, Inc., Publishers, New York.

Routledge & Kegan Paul Ltd. and Basic Books, Inc., Publishers, for *The Child's Conception of Movement and Speed*, by Jean Piaget. Translated from the French by G. E. T. Holloway and M. J. MacKenzie. English translation copyright © 1970 by Routledge & Kegan Paul Ltd. and Basic Books, Inc., Publishers, New York.

Routledge & Kegan Paul Ltd. and W. W. Norton & Company, Inc., for *Play, Dreams and Imitation in Childhood*, by Jean Piaget. Translated by C. Gattegno and F. M. Hodgson. All rights reserved. W. W. Norton & Company, Inc. Norton Library Edition 1962.

Routledge & Kegan Paul Ltd. and The Free Press for *The Moral Judgment of the Child*, by Jean Piaget. Reprinted with permission of the Macmillan Company, first published 1932.

STANDARD BOOK NUMBER: 06–013439–9

LIBRARY OF CONGRESS CATALOG CARD NUMBER: 79–138758

Designed by Charlotte Thorp

To my children
SANDY and BETSY
and to all children growing up today

contents

introduction

Why should one wish to read about the psychological theories of Jean Piaget? Because he is one of the most influential of living thinkers. His ideas about the development of cognition in children are affecting research, curriculum planning, preschool programs, and many other areas of psychology and education today. Just as Freud opened our eyes to children's emotional growth, so Piaget is casting new light on our understanding of children's intellectual growth. Thinking, knowing, perceiving, remembering, recognizing, abstracting, generalizing—all these processes are included in the term "cognition," which refers to all the intellective activities of the mind. Piaget's studies of cognitive development help us to understand what to expect of children, how they perceive the world around them at different ages, and why they ask questions and interpret information in ways that seem strange to adults.

Piaget is a Swiss psychologist who has been working with children for half a century. He is interested in how children learn to know, how they order their thinking. How does a baby come to recognize his mother, for example, and to know who are strangers? When and by what steps does a child learn to add and manipulate numbers? How does he develop language? What is the relation between maturation and learning? These are questions Piaget has tried to answer with results that have had a growing impact on present-day psychology. His early works, translated into English in the 1920's, were received with astonishment and disbelief. A good deal of criticism followed because of the small number of subjects studied and the lack of statistical validation; in his early work Piaget ignored most of the accepted methods of scientific research. For many years his contributions were largely neglected in this country, but since about 1950 there has been a tremendous revival of interest in his work. Most of his numerous books have been published in English, and a growing body of research is developing, based on his findings.

If Piaget's thinking is so important, why not read it in the original? Because Piaget has been publishing prolifically ever since he was ten, and it has become a monumental task to keep up with all his productions. He is the author of close to thirty books and innumerable articles in the field of child development alone. Moreover, his ideas, like Freud's, have grown and changed with the years, so that his later theories are more developed or have different areas of emphasis from those of his early works. In addition, Piaget writes in French, and his terms are sometimes translated differently by different scholars. This makes it difficult to follow his thinking from one book to another.

Even if all Piaget's work were available in one volume by one translator, the uninitiated would find it hard to understand. Piaget uses very difficult terms, such as *reciprocal assimilation* and *genetic epistemology*. Furthermore, he employs familiar words such as "conservation" and "egocentrism" with shades of meaning which are different from their usual connotation. In this book I have attempted to avoid such terminology as much as possible, in an effort to make Piaget's thinking and research understandable to everyone interested in children. I hope readers will share my enjoyment of his deep insight, his warm empathy for children, and his quiet sense of humor. The mark of Piaget's greatness is that his ideas are so fruitful and have generated so much interest and research among others. He has broken fresh ground and gleaned a rich harvest of knowledge. There are many who feel that Piaget will eventually be as well known as Freud. Already his influence has been so profound that today no knowledgeable person can afford to be unfamiliar with his ideas.

Piaget's research is so comprehensive and so fully developed that a guide is needed in approaching it. This book attempts to fill that need. First, it reviews the theoretical rationale behind Piaget's work and sets forth his basic principles of development. Then comes an overview of developmental stages of intellectual growth from infancy to adolescence. Next, there follows a more detailed presentation of Piaget's work in many different areas, including his studies of time, speed, and perception, which have only recently been translated. Piaget's views on education and teacher training serve to sum up the impact of his thinking on child psychology today.

For those who wish to go further in the study of Piaget, there follows a special bibliography, which includes a number of books about Piaget and reports of research based on his theories. These appear constantly, in the journals of child development and genetic psychology, and the author cannot pretend to keep up with them. However, several edited collections are listed here.

For those who wish to read Piaget's own works, a chronological listing by French publication dates is included with acknowledgments to Henry Maier, whose previous listing this author consulted. Such a chronology is necessary because the English translations do not correspond to the times or order in which the originals were written. The first five books belong in Piaget's early period, when he was interested in the conversations, questions, and reasoning of the preschool children he saw at the Maison des Petits. We might call this his preoperational period. His second period includes three books based on his own children. They study the very beginnings of intelligence in babies and show how children develop their earliest notions of time, space, causality, and object constancy during the sensory-motor period. Since about 1940, Piaget has been developing his theories of grouping and the logical expression of cognitive structures. His works on logic, perception, time, speed, and number are all characterized by these logico-mathematical formulations; we might call this his operational period.

We have reviewed all of these, as well as most of the earlier books, which are better known and more easily read. In addition there are a number of articles which have appeared in journals such as *Scientific American,* or in edited collections. Some of these, such as "Children's Philosophies," are delightful reading. The reader, however, must be aware of the time sequence of Piaget's work. In a recent contribution (to Mussen [ed.], *Carmichael's Manual of Child Psychology*) he explains that his theory has never been completed and that he considers himself one of the chief "revisionists of Piaget."

Reading Piaget over the years, one notes a major change. Instead of the earlier, rather mechanical formulation of stages and substages, he has developed an increasing awareness of the complex interactions taking place between the child and his environment. Out of this interaction develop the structures of thought, each one richer, more complex, more inclusive than the one before. This recapitulation of intellectual development at each succeeding stage is a fascinating aspect of cognitive growth.

In writing this guide to Piaget's work, I am indebted to many people. I have drawn heavily on Dr. John Flavell's *Developmental Psychology of Jean Piaget*, a comprehensive and scholarly text which was my first introduction to Piaget. I am also indebted to Dr. David Elkind for his delightful and lucid essays interpreting Piaget. Dr. Wayne Dennis of Brooklyn College (now retired) was the professor who first sparked my interest in Piaget; for his consistent encouragement and his corrections of the manuscript I am most grateful. Other readers who have made very helpful suggestions are Dr. Deanna Kuhn of Columbia University and Dr. Doreen Berman of the City University of New York. Mrs. Harriet Carlin and Mrs. Josephine Pearce have shown me how to apply Piaget's theories in the classroom. My editor, Mrs. Ann Harris of Harper & Row, has constantly smoothed the way and made working with her a pleasure. Mrs. Margit Breakiron put aside her portraits of children to do many of the illustrations for this book. Miss Catherine E. Sandy and the staff of the Port Washington Public Library were most helpful in locating hard-to-find references. Finally, the manuscript would never have been published were it not for the care and efficiency of Mrs. Aline Smith, who typed it. To all of them, and most especially to my forebearing husband I extend my grateful thanks.

M.A.P.

1

Piaget: a profile

Jean Piaget was born on August 9, 1896, in Neuchâtel, Switzerland. His father was a scholar of medieval history, "a man of painstaking and critical mind"[1]* who passed on to his little boy the habit of systematic thinking down to the least detail which is so apparent in Piaget's writings. His mother was very intelligent and devoutly religious. Piaget reports in his autobiography that "her rather neurotic temperament . . . made our family life somewhat troublesome."[2] As a consequence of the atmosphere at home, Piaget reports that he early became a serious little boy, interested in mechanics, birds, fossils, and sea shells. At the age of ten he published his first paper on a partly albino sparrow he had seen in the park. Then he asked the director of the natural history museum in Neuchâtel if he

* Notes begin on page 213.

might assist him after school hours. This kindly man put the boy to work labeling his extensive collection of shells. The director was a specialist in mollusks, and he taught the eager youngster a great deal, as well as giving him rare specimens for his own collection.

After four years of this association, the director died; but Piaget had learned enough to begin publishing articles on malacology (the branch of zoology dealing with mollusks) in the zoological journals. As a result of these, he was offered the position of curator of the mollusk collection by the director of the museum of natural history in Geneva—a position he was forced to decline because he was still a schoolboy. Piaget went on to take his degree in the natural sciences at the University of Neuchâtel and in 1918 was awarded a doctorate for his thesis on malacology. His childish curiosity about mollusks had developed into an abiding interest in biology, which was to influence Piaget's thinking for the rest of his life.

During his adolescent years Piaget read extensively in philosophy, religion, sociology, and psychology. His godfather introduced him to Henri Bergson's philosophy of creative evolution, and Piaget reports, "The identification of God with life itself was an idea that stirred me almost to ecstasy because it now enabled me to see in biology the explanation for all things and of the mind itself."[3] The young scientist decided at that moment to consecrate his life to the biological explanation of knowledge. The problem of knowledge—the epistemological problem of how and what we know—is one that has challenged philosophers down through the ages. But between this philosophical problem and its biological substrate there was a missing link—the human mind. This, Piaget later realized, could only be understood through psychology. For it is the mind which knows, and the mind is based in the body and is subject to the laws of heredity. Thus Piaget conceived the term *genetic epistemology* to express his idea that intellectual development—how we come to know—is firmly rooted in the biological development of the individual, as expressed by the term "genetic." To this day Piaget regards himself not as a psychologist but as a geneticist whose main interest is in the development of knowledge.

Because of his mother's poor mental health, Piaget also became intensely interested in psychopathology and the theories of Freud. After completing his doctorate he worked for a year in Eugen Bleuler's psychiatric clinic in Zurich; there he learned the art of clinical interviewing which would later serve him well in his questioning of young children. Then Piaget went on to Paris to study at the Sorbonne for two years. While there, he became acquainted with Théophile Simon, coauthor with Alfred Binet of the first intelligence test. Dr. Simon suggested that Piaget standardize Cyril Burt's reasoning tests, used as part of the Binet scale, on Parisian children.

These tests consist of questions involving part-whole relationships, such as: "Some of my flowers are buttercups. Does my bouquet contain (1) all yellow flowers; (2) some yellow flowers; (3) no yellow flowers?" Questions like these, Piaget discovered, were very hard for children under eleven or twelve because they have difficulty understanding the relationship of the part (yellow flowers) to the whole (bouquet). He found himself becoming more interested in why children fail tests such as these than in establishing norms for success. By what paths did children reach their answers? What thought processes led them astray? What factors did they fail to grasp in their search for solutions? To answer these questions, Piaget began to study the reasoning of children. He presented them with "open-ended" questions about relationships or problems of cause and effect. His findings were then published in a series of articles.

One of these articles drew the attention of Dr. Edouard Claparéde, director of the Institut Jean Jacques Rousseau in Geneva, a school formed for the scientific study of the child and the training of teachers. Claparéde offered Piaget the position of director of research at this institute. He accepted, and in 1921, at the age of twenty-five, the young biologist, now become a psychologist, embarked on the research that was to be his life's work.

During the next decade Piaget published five books based on his research with children at the Maison des Petits, the preschool of the Institut Jean Jacques Rousseau. These brought him world-wide attention and made him famous before he was thirty. He also married one of his students at the institute, and in time they had three children—Jacqueline, Lucienne, and Laurent. With his wife's help Piaget studied their cognitive development in careful detail; on these observations he based his later books on the development of intelligence during infancy and toddlerhood.

As he extended his studies into childhood and adolescence, he collaborated with others, notably Alina Szeminska and Bärbel Inhelder, on books on the development of logical thinking in regard to numbers, geometry, space, time, and quantity. Piaget also became very much interested in the development of perception in children and published a whole series of articles on this subject.

During this time Piaget taught courses in philosophy, psychology, and sociology at the institute and at the Universities of Geneva, Neuchâtel, and Lausanne. In 1929 he was appointed a director of the International Board of Education. After the war he gave generously of his time to UNESCO and became a member of its executive council. He has received many honors, including more than a dozen honorary degrees from universities in many countries. Today Piaget is the director of his own research institute, the International Center of Genetic Epistemology, as well as co-director of the Institute of Educational Science. Students from all over the world come to Geneva to study with him. In 1950 he published his theory of knowledge, which summarizes in three volumes the work of a lifetime. Now, in his seventies, he is still actively researching and thinking.

Dr. David Elkind, a psychologist who spent a year working with Piaget, describes his schedule as follows:

Piaget's is a superbly disciplined life. He arises early each morning, sometimes as early as 4 A.M., and writes four or more publishable pages on square sheets of white paper in a small, even hand. Later in the morning he may teach classes and attend meetings. His afternoons include long walks during which he thinks about the problems he is currently confronting. He says, "I always like to think on a problem before reading about it." In the evenings he reads and retires early. Even on his international trips, Piaget keeps to this schedule.[4]

During the summers, says Elkind, Piaget takes all his materials and retreats to an abandoned farmhouse in the Alps where he walks, thinks, and writes prodigiously. In the fall he leaves his secret hideaway and returns to the world of research, teaching, and public responsibilities. With a beret over his snowy hair, a pipe in his mouth, and a twinkle in his eye, he is a familiar figure around the streets of Geneva. And as more and more research bears out his theories, his ideas are becoming familiar around the world.

2

adaptation: the basis of behavior

Adaptation is for Piaget the essence of intellectual functioning, just as it is the essence of biological functioning. We have long been familiar with adaptation in the Darwinian sense of "survival of the fittest." But to Piaget the word means more than just survival; it means modifying the environment to our own ends. He believes that an essential part of our biological inheritance is a mode of intellectual functioning which remains constant throughout life. This functioning is characterized by the ability to organize the myriad sensations and experiences we encounter into some kind of order, and to adapt ourselves to our surroundings.

The cave men who were terrified by fire ran from it and hid; thus they survived. Later they learned to control it, so that it provided them with warmth, cooked food, and protection from animals. By making it work for them they displayed intelligent, adaptive functioning. Such functioning, according to Piaget, is characteristic of living organisms at all levels; it is part of our biological inheritance.

Adaptation has a dual nature; it consists of twin processes which go on continuously in all living organisms. *Assimilation* is the taking-in process, whether of sensation, nourishment, or experience. It is the process by which one incorporates things, people, ideas, customs, and tastes into one's own activity. For example, a child, listening to people talking around him, learns the inflections, the phrasing, and the meaning of language long before he is able to talk himself. He is assimilating everything he hears, and gradually making it his own.

Assimilation is continuously balanced by *accommodation,* the outgoing, adjusting process of reaching out to the environment. Thus the listening child begins to babble in response to conversation around him and gradually approximates the words he has assimilated. "Daddy" comes out "da-da," and "flower" may be "fwodder," but as the child continues his efforts, he accommodates his words to those he hears, and his baby talk becomes understandable speech. Thus he adapts to the language requirements of his environment.

These two processes, functioning simultaneously at all biological and intellectual levels, make possible both physical and cognitive development. As an example, consider Piaget's beloved mollusks, which are among the more primitive organisms. They accommodate to the rough waters of the lake of Neuchâtel, he reports, by clamping themselves to the stones, and there they assimilate whatever food comes floating by. We see the same processes operating in the human baby who is learning to take his first solid food from a spoon. He must learn to assimilate it by licking and chewing rather than by his previous method of sucking. At the same time he must open his mouth and accommodate to the size and position of the spoon, rather than the nipple he is used to. In this way he adapts to a new experience.

The same thing happens when the baby receives his first rattle. He tries to assimilate it into his mouth, meanwhile accommodating his mouth to his plaything's size and shape. But this experience produces a cognitive rather than a digestive adaptation. The baby learns that this is a suckable but not a swallowable object, and henceforth modifies his concept of objects-that-go-in-the-mouth to include two subcategories: (1) edible objects and (2) nonedible objects. Later on, after he has heard "No, no!" enough times, he will learn that there are objects which do *not* go in the mouth, as well as those that do. Eventually, to use Piaget's term, the *schema* of food will be clearly differentiated from other *schemata* (plural) or concepts or categories of experience such as toys or Mother's cigarette.

Thus, while functioning adaptively, the baby is also developing intellectually. He is organizing his new experiences in various ways—differentiating, integrating, categorizing—so that the first vague global schema of objects-that-go-in-the-mouth becomes sophisticated and complex enough to include all the varied members of the category "food." We see also that in Piaget's developmental psychology the baby is never a passive, helpless infant as some psychologists picture him, reacting only to loud noises and loss of support. He is an active and curious organism, reaching out, experimenting, seeking always to maintain a stable balance between assimilation and accommodation, between his inner reality and that of the world around him. Just as the body seeks to find a physiological state of equilibrium between exercise and rest, or hunger and overeating, so the child's mind seeks equilibrium between what he understands and what he experiences in his environment.

This process of seeking mental equilibrium Piaget calls

equilibration. Its function is to bring about a balanced co-ordination between assimilation and accommodation, just as a thermostat maintains a constant balance between heat and cold. He conceives of this process as the mechanism for growth and transition in cognitive development. "In a sense," he writes, "development is a progressive equilibration from a lesser to a higher state of equilibrium."[1] The mind seeks to understand and to explain at all levels, but the vague, incoherent explanations of childhood are a far cry from the systematized logic of adult reasoning. It is the search for equilibrium, for answers that satisfy, which spurs the mind on to higher levels of thought.

But once the organism is in equilibrium, what upsets it? What stimulates the child to achieve higher stages of cognitive development? Why and how does he learn? In answering these questions Piaget recognizes first of all the dynamic factor of *maturation.* As the schemata or cognitive structures develop, the child begins to use them just as he uses his developing muscles to walk, and then to run and climb. Piaget stresses very strongly the importance of maturation in mental as well as in physical development. A child is not capable of thinking like an adult because he simply does not have the logical structures, the organizations of thought, and the methods of reasoning which would enable him to deal with adult problems. This is why you cannot teach calculus to a five-year-old, says Piaget; he simply doesn't have the structures of thought to assimilate it. But as he grows and matures, his mind becomes increasingly alert and active. As any parent who has lived through the "Why, Daddy?" stage can attest, the child becomes curious about many things. He explores and experiments until he finds an answer that satisfies him, and achieves equilibrium, at least for that stage of his development.

The second factor that Piaget calls upon to explain cognitive development is *experience*. By this he means physical and empirical experience such as the child encounters while floating boats, flying kites, counting objects, and lifting weights. This is the kind of direct sensory-motor experience which is lacking among many urban children today and must be supplied by Head Start and "extended readiness" programs. The child who has never seen or smelled a fresh orange (because his mother buys frozen juice), who has never learned to climb a tree or balance himself on a railing, has missed some of the tremendously complex sensory and motor experiences that go to make up the background for school learning. For such a child, pictures of trees and oranges in a book do not have much meaning. He must go back and explore the rich world of childhood—touching, smelling, climbing, digging—before he is ready to settle down to books full of squiggly, meaningless symbols called "letters."

Piaget is fond of telling the story of a friend of his, a mathematician whose career began with an experience in early childhood. One day when he was four or five, he was sitting on the ground in his garden playing with pebbles. He arranged them in a row and counted, one, two, three, up to ten. Then he counted them backwards, and once again there were ten pebbles! With increasing excitement he arranged them in a circle, and in various other ways, always with the same result. He had made the marvelous discovery that the sum is independent of the order. For him the transition to arithmetic and then higher mathematics would come without difficulty, his growing understanding built upon this simple but meaningful childhood experience. This is why Piaget insists that children must be allowed to do their own learning. Thoughts, or "mental operations," to use his term, arise out of motor actions and sensory experiences which are "interiorized." The child who has had physical experience with a concrete object such as a ball can then form a mental image of that object and act upon it in thought as he has in actual experiences in the past. He can think about throwing the ball, and his thought is "interiorized action." But the child who has never handled or thrown a ball is handicapped in his intellectual development. Teachers and parents of young children will recognize here a plea for enriched experience at the sensory-motor level, rather than accelerated learning brought about by what Piaget calls the "pedagogical mania" of adults.

A third factor contributing to equilibration is what Piaget calls *social transmission*— the verbal instructions transmitted by parents and teachers in the process of education. He believes that when a child hears contradictory or challenging statements, whether at home or in school, his equilibrium is disturbed. He then sets out in search of an answer which will enable him to achieve a new and higher equilibrium. One of Piaget's students has coined the term "cognitive conflict" for these states of disturbed equilibrium. When an organism is thrown into a state of cognitive conflict it searches for a solution like a small boy trying to find out whether or not there is a Santa Claus. When he was younger, he believed in Santa Claus, but now he suddenly begins to notice that there is one on every street corner. Or his siblings tell him there is no such person, and he is disturbed and troubled until he finds an explanation that makes sense to him in his new, less naïve state of development. Thus, as the child's mental structures become capable of grappling with new problems, he is stimulated and challenged by his environment to seek new solutions. His cognitive conflict spurs him on to higher levels of intellectual development; or to put it oversimply, he learns from his mistakes.

For Piaget, adaptive functioning is constant at all levels of development, although the mental structures, ideas, or concepts characteristic of different states of equilibrium may vary widely from one state to another. As we follow him in his efforts to observe and describe the various stages in cognitive development which are common to all children, we see why Piaget's ideas are having such a profound effect on present-day psychology. He sees the child not as a miniature adult, but as living in a world that is completely different from ours, and sometimes quite incomprehensible to us. He is interested not in individual differences but in the constancy of modes of conceptualization for children of all races and periods of history. All children, he says, must go through certain stages of intellectual development in the same order. Bright children may develop more quickly than dull ones, but the progression from stage to stage is the same for every child as he learns to adapt to the world around him. As the evidence comes in from studies of children in many different countries, it provides strong support for Piaget's theory of a constant sequence of stages in intellectual development.[2]

3

the beginnings of intelligence

Babies come alive when one reads Piaget. Suddenly that helpless, red-faced infant, alternately squalling or sleeping, becomes
a complex, fascinating organism, groping in a bewildering environment not only to survive but to comprehend and control.
Piaget watches intently as the baby struggles to focus on a
swinging watch or a familiar voice, and systematically records
his results. Each of his many observations is minutely and
precisely detailed, numbered, and labeled as to the child's age:
e.g., 0;6(12) means no years, 6 months, and 12 days. Reading
them, one wonders how Piaget found time to do anything else,
he sounds so absorbed in watching his children:

Observation 77. At 0;6(0) Jacqueline looks at my watch, which
is 10 cm. from her eyes. She reveals a lively interest, and her hands
flutter as though she were about to grasp; without however dis-

covering the right direction. I place the watch in her right hand without her being able to see how (the arm being outstretched). Then I again put the watch before her eyes. Her hands, apparently excited by the contact just experienced, then proceed to move through space and meet violently, subsequently to separate. The right hand happens to strike the watch; Jacqueline immediately tries to adjust her hand to the watch and thus manages to grasp it. The experiment is repeated three times: it is always when the hand is perceived at the same time as the watch that the attempts become systematic. The next day, at 0;6(1) I resume the experiment. When the watch is before her eyes, Jacqueline does not attempt to grasp it although she reveals a lively interest in this object. When the watch is near her hand and she happens to touch it, or it is seen at the same time as her hand, then there is searching, and searching directed by the glance. Near the eyes and far from the hands the watch is again simply contemplated. The hands move a little but do not approach each other. I again place the object near her hand: immediate searching, and again success. I put the watch a third time a few centimeters from her eyes and far from her hands: these move in all directions but without approaching each other. In short there are still two worlds for Jacqueline, one kinesthetic and the other visual. It is only when the object is seen next to the hand that the latter is directed toward it and manages to grasp it. That evening, the same experiment with various solid objects. Again and very regularly, when Jacqueline sees the object facing her without perceiving her hands, nothing happens, whereas the simultaneous sight of object and of hand (right or left) sets prehension in motion. Finally it is to be noted that, that day, Jacqueline again watched with great interest her empty hand crossing the visual field: the hand is still not felt to belong to her.[1]

It is on hundreds of careful observations such as this that Piaget bases his theory of the cognitive development of infants. The results of his investigations form an important part of his genetic theory of knowledge. The behavior of babies, says Piaget, like that of all biological organisms, exemplifies the continuously functioning process of adaptation. Intelligence is an integral part of that adaptation. Just as the infant's respiration, digestion, and motor coordination function to adapt him to the environment, so his intelligence functions to make him increasingly master of his world. But though intelligent functioning is constant and does not change, the mental structures through which it manifests itself do; they grow and develop from age to age, giving rise to Piaget's theory of stages. This has been much misunderstood; critics have tended to attack Piaget because they disagreed with the specific ages at which he stated certain behaviors would occur. The important point is not that children do certain things at certain ages, but that they go through certain stages of development in a regular, continuous sequence, each stage arising out of the preceding one and building upon it not only larger but more complex structures. "From this point of view," says Piaget, "mental development is a continuous construction comparable to the erection of a vast building that becomes more solid with each addition."[2] Unlike a building, however, intellectual development is flexible, supple, and mobile, seeking always for adjustment resulting in equilibrium.

Piaget puts a great deal of emphasis upon classifying behavior into discrete stages. This may be due to his early museum training and classificatory zeal; or it may represent an earnest effort at clarification of the steps involved in development. It seems a little too good to be true that all sensory-motor behavior, whether in reference to objects, space, time, or causality, should fit neatly into six stages of development. However, whether the development of babies actually occurs in just these stages, or whether they represent mental structures imposed by Piaget in the process of organizing his wealth of observations, is not relevant here. The behaviors that he observed do provide milestones in cognitive development, just as do the first tooth and the first steps in physical development. Piaget would certainly agree that development is a continuous,

ongoing process which manifests itself through gradually increasing complexity, differentiation, and enrichment from one
stage to the next. Rather than thinking of stages as steps in
development, one might conceive of them as part of a continuous, upward-growing, ever widening spiral, each loop growing out of the preceding one and merging into that which
follows, yet each one observable apart from the others.

Piaget's use of the term *stages* is confusing, since it differs
from earlier to later works. The detailed development of infants followed here is taken from *The Origins of Intelligence in
Children,* which is based on Piaget's observations in the 1930's
of his own three children. In later discussions[3] he uses different
classificatory schemes, but all the developments described below are included in his discussion of the first two years of
childhood. He calls this the *sensory-motor* period, extending
from birth to one and a half or two years. This is followed by
three more advanced periods which will be discussed in Chapter 4. However, these periods of development are often referred to as stages, in which case the stages which follow below
must be thought of as substages occurring during the larger
stage or period of development.

Piaget calls this earliest period of cognitive development the
sensory-motor period because the infant's earliest manifesta-
tions of intelligence appear in his sensory perceptions and his
motor activities. His eyes follow a moving object; his head
turns in response to a noise; he begins to reach for and grasp
his toys. These may appear to be small achievements, and many
parents do not find tiny babies interesting. Yet Piaget points
out that the child in his first two years effects "a miniature
Copernican revolution."[4] He is at first helpless, unaware of the
world around him, conscious only of himself—the center of
his own small universe. As he grows and reaches outward, both
mentally and physically, he becomes aware of other people, of

the world around him, of objects that exist independently of him. By the time he is two, he is aware of himself as part of a larger family, a larger world. He takes his place in a universe which he experiences as external to himself. This is no small achievement.

At birth, says Piaget, the infant is "locked in egocentrism." By this he means not that the baby is self-centered but that he is unaware of anything beyond himself. He knows nothing of the world apart from his immediate consciousness and therefore cannot at first distinguish himself from it or make any sense out of the variety of stimuli he receives from it. He comes into the world equipped with a few neonatal reflexes such as sucking and grasping which are part of his biological inheritance. Beyond these, his behavior consists of gross motor movements, uncoordinated and purposeless. His feet kick, his hands wave, his eyes do not focus. But sometime after the first month the baby's fist accidentally finds its way into his mouth. By reflex action he begins to suck on it and apparently finds this activity satisfying. At any rate, the baby repeats this action over and over again until he learns to bring his fist to his mouth at will. After that, not only his fist but everything else he grasps will find its way into his mouth. "For him," says Piaget, "the world is essentially a thing to be sucked."[5] This development marks the transition from the first stage of simple hereditary reflexes to the second stage of learned or "acquired adaptations" (one to four months). He has put together two separate actions—fist waving and sucking—to form a new behavior pattern or schema of bringing the fist to the mouth to be sucked.

In the third stage (four to eight months) the child turns from movements centered on himself to respond to something in the external environment. A more complicated "circular reaction" occurs when the baby seeks to maintain an interesting change in the environment which he produced accidentally.

He may bump a rattle, and when it makes a noise, he moves around and explores until he bumps it again.

Observation 95. Lucienne, at 0;4(27) is lying in her bassinet. I hang a doll over her feet which immediately sets in motion the schema of [shaking]. . . . But her feet reach the doll right away and give it a violent movement which Lucienne surveys with delight. Afterward she looks at her motionless foot for a second, then recommences. There is no visual control of the foot, for the movements are the same when Lucienne only looks at the doll or when I place the doll over her head. On the other hand, the tactile control of the foot is apparent: after the first shakes, Lucienne makes slow foot movements as though to grasp and explore. For instance, when she tries to kick the doll and misses her aim, she begins again very slowly until she succeeds (without seeing her feet). In the same way I cover Lucienne's face or distract her attention for a moment in another direction; she nevertheless continues to hit the doll and control its movements.[6]

Here Lucienne is intentionally adapting, in order to repeat a response which she finds new and interesting. Already she is becoming a curious little explorer who repeats actions that please her until she has mastered them. Her active efforts to re-create the interesting response show that she is capable of anticipation and the beginnings of intentional, goal-directed behavior. But she still has difficulty coordinating these efforts because the various schemata such as vision and prehension are not yet fully coordinated. As Piaget noted in his observation of Jacqueline (see Chapter 2), her eyes and her hands were in different spheres, and she could not use them together.

The fourth stage (eight to twelve months) is characterized by the emergence of intentional behavior. The child pushes aside an obstacle which prevents him from reaching something he wants. He may use his parent's hand to get something which he can see but cannot reach himself.

At 0;7(10) Laurent tries to grasp a new box in front of which I place my hand (at a distance of 10 cm.). He sets the obstacle aside, but not intentionally; he simply tries to reach the box by sliding next to my hand and, when he touches it, tries to take no notice of it. This behavior gives the impression that he pushes the screen away, but there does not yet exist any differentiated schema, any "means" dissociated from the final action (from the schema assigning an end to the action). The behavior pattern is the same when I use a cushion as an obstacle.

Same reactions at 0;7(12). Finally, at 0;7(13) Laurent reacts quite differently almost from the beginning of the experiment. I present a box of matches above my hand, but behind it, so that he cannot reach it without setting the obstacle aside. But Laurent, after trying to take no notice of it, suddenly tries to hit my hand as though to remove or lower it; I let him do it to me and he grasps the box. I recommence to bar his passage, but using as a screen a sufficiently supple cushion to keep the impress of the child's gestures. Laurent tries to reach the box, and, bothered by the obstacle, he at once strikes it, definitely lowering it until the way is clear.[7]

If a desired object is hidden, however, the child acts as though it no longer existed. Piaget explains that the baby has not yet developed *object constancy;* he does not know that objects exist in the environment even when he does not see them. This is a manifestation of Piaget's term *egocentrism;* the baby is aware only of his immediate experience. If that experience does not include perceiving the object, then he has no idea that the object is there and has permanence of its own. It is only gradually, after a good deal of experience with objects that swing or drop or roll out of sight, that the child looks for them, indicating that he now knows they are there. In this stage babies also begin to anticipate events and respond to cues such as the sound of a mother's voice even when she is still out of sight. Games such as "peekaboo" or "hide-and-seek" now become a source of unfailing delight because of the reappearance of the hidden but expected object. Such activities help to establish in the child the notion of object constancy or permanence, one of the major achievements of the sensory-motor period. An essential for later learning, this realization of the permanence of objects reduces the child's egocentrism by enabling him to differentiate between himself and external reality which exists independently of him.

The fifth stage (twelve to eighteen months) is marked by the emergence of what Piaget calls *directed groping*. The child begins to experiment in order to see what will happen. No longer does he simply repeat movements in order to produce a desired result. Now he begins to vary his movements as if to observe how the results will differ. Piaget describes his little son Laurent breaking off one piece of bread at a time and dropping it on the floor, watching with great interest to see where it would fall. The average parent would probably take the bread away in annoyance; but Piaget waited quietly, noting the child's absorbed attention. Like a serious young Galileo, the little boy dropped the bread from various positions and watched it land in different places on the floor. Piaget considers this behavior experimental; it differs from that of the preceding stage in that it is not a stereotyped repetition of behavior but introduces experimental variations as if to see what will happen.

Another development of this stage is that the child learns to use new means to achieve an end. He discovers that he can pull objects to him by a string or a stick, or tilt them to get them through the bars of his playpen. In other words, his trial-and-error behavior is directed toward a goal; the child is functioning intelligently.

Observation 155. At 1;0(26) in Jacqueline's presence I place my watch on the floor, beyond her field of prehension. I put the chain in a straight line in Jacqueline's direction but place a cushion on the part which is nearest the child. Jacqueline at first tries to grasp the watch directly. Not succeeding, she looks at the chain. She notes that the latter is under the cushion. Then Jacqueline removes the

Figure 1

latter at one stroke and pulls the chain while looking at the watch. The movement is adapted and quick. As soon as the watch is within reach, Jacqueline lets go of the chain in order to grasp the object directly. There is, consequently, no interest in the chain itself; it is the watch that is wanted.[8]

In the sixth and last stage of sensory-motor behavior (eighteen months to one and a half or two years) the child begins to do his groping mentally rather than physically. As Piaget puts it, the child's physical or motor action is "interiorized"; the child *thinks* about how he would do something without actually doing it, until he reaches a satisfactory solution. Piaget calls this "the invention of new means" and says that it develops along with symbolic representation. The child at this stage is making the transition from physical to mental operations or thought and can represent actions in a symbolic way without actually performing them.

Piaget loves to describe how he played with Lucienne when she was sixteen months old by hiding his watch chain in a matchbox. First he left the matchbox open wide enough so that the little girl could get her fingers in and pull out the chain. Then Piaget, keeping his movements out of the child's sight, closed the box except for a small slit, too narrow for Lucienne's eager fingers. A pause followed, says Piaget, during which Lucienne showed that she tried to think out the situation and represent to herself what she must do. She looked at the slit with great attention; she opened her mouth slightly, then wider and wider, mimicking with her mouth what she wished to do to the matchbox. Then she unhesitatingly grasped the box, put her index finger into the slit, and pulled it open wide enough to take out the chain. Piaget says that since Lucienne could not yet think out the situation clearly, she represented it symbolically by her motor imitation of the desired act. By opening her mouth she represented to herself how she could open the box. Lucienne was on the verge of thought!

Thus, in six easy stages Piaget shows us how the infant develops from a biological organism into a social one. He traces the growth of cognition from the first primitive reflex to the complex and varied combinations of behavior soon to be telescoped in thought. Always there is the upward spiraling of development. The various behavior patterns are repeated over and over until they are mastered; then, propelled by the hierarchic movement of growth, they occur again in new and more complicated forms. In two years or less the child has completed the Copernican revolution which Piaget described. He has achieved, first of all, the notion of object constancy, the realization that objects and people have a permanent existence which is independent of his perception of them. He has also developed a primitive notion of causality, for he has discovered that certain actions of his produce certain results. In his experimenting with objects he has acquired rudimentary concepts of space and time; he can locate his toys and knows that daily events have a certain sequence. All of these discoveries have helped to increase his awareness of himself as separate from other people, thereby decreasing his egocentrism. He has begun to retain mental images beyond his immediate sensory experience and can anticipate coming events. In other words, he has reached the level of development achieved by the highest animals. A mature chimpanzee can manipulate objects and reach for bananas with a stick. A dog can fetch his leash as a symbolic indication that he wants to go for a walk. But the child is now ready to surpass the achievements of any animal. In two years he has come a long way.

4

an overview of development

We have already traced the baby's growth from the stage of neonatal reflexes (present at birth) to the development of symbolic images. We will now summarize the later periods of development briefly, before going on to study them in greater depth.

SENSORY-MOTOR PERIOD
(FIRST TWO YEARS)

A brief summary of the six stages of the baby's development appears in outline form in Appendix A.

PREOPERATIONAL PERIOD
(TWO TO SEVEN YEARS)

During the preschool years the child must bridge the gap between the sensory-motor activities of the baby and the internal mental activities or *operations* of the school-age child. He does this gradually, as we shall see in the studies of conservation, responding first to the primacy of sensations ("It looks bigger, therefore it must be bigger"). Only much later, after considerable experience, does he become aware of the logical necessity of rationally apprehended facts. A little child does not "see" that two rows of three buttons is the same as three rows of two buttons. First he must count the buttons many times, until the experience becomes internalized, and he "gets" it. This is to say he grasps the information on a logical or mental level and no longer needs the physical experience of counting the buttons.

The child in the preoperational period learns to use symbolic substitutes such as language, and mental images, for the sensory-motor activities of infancy. Instead of grasping, he can ask for things. Instead of seeing his mother he can think of her and can thus get along without her immediate presence for longer periods of time. Piaget feels that the "make-believe" play of this period is very important, because through it the child is assimilating symbolically the activities, roles, and ideas of the world around him. Jacqueline drank out of a shell as if it were a glass; Lucienne gave her doll an orange peel to eat and called it macaroni. In so doing, the little girls were using symbols for dishes and food, and through their make-believe were assimilating and consolidating as part of their experience the customs and manners observed in their environment. At the same time, this assimilation was being balanced by accommodation, which Piaget describes as being the primary function of imitation. By imitating the speech, the behavior, the activities of adults, children learn to adjust to new situations in their world. Who has not observed the behavior of children after the first days of kindergarten? They come home and immediately start "playing school." By imitating the teacher and the activities of the classroom they are able to accommodate to a new and strange situation. At the same time, by making "school" into a symbolic game they are assimilating it, relating it to experiences already familiar to them in the past.

The characteristics of this period and the periods following it will be discussed at length in following sections. This section aims to give first a brief overview of all of Piaget's developmental periods.

PERIOD OF CONCRETE OPERATIONS
(SEVEN TO ELEVEN OR TWELVE YEARS)

Piaget is fond of pointing out that thought processes in the operational period are speeded up like a movie film, as compared to the slow-motion succession of slides in preoperational functioning. Operations or thoughts, freed from the bondage of physical performance, can short-circuit with amazing rapidity. Thought can project itself forward into time and space or reverse itself like a movie being rewound. Thought can be communicated more easily, too, as a result of the development of language. The term *concrete operations* means that the child can now operate in thought on concrete objects or their representations. He can serialize, extend, subdivide, differentiate, or combine existing structures into new relationships or groupings. He now thinks logically about things rather than accepting surface appearances. But his thought is still limited to his own concrete experiences; he is not yet capable of dealing with abstractions such as "billions of years" which are logically possible but cannot be conceived in concrete, realistic terms.

Piaget attempted to discover all the properties of thought operations or groupings observed in the grade-school child and to express them in the language of logic and mathematics. His work on this level is much more difficult to read and understand than his books on young children. However, his description of the properties of children's thought during the school years has been extremely important in stimulating research and discussion and has influenced many areas of curriculum planning. A fuller discussion of cognitive development at this age level follows in Chapter 7.

PERIOD OF FORMAL OPERATIONS
(ELEVEN OR TWELVE YEARS ON)

The last period of cognitive development described by Piaget appears in early adolescence. The youngster now begins to "operate on operations," which means he can think about thought rather than about concrete things. Formal operations are called "operations to the second order"; they concern the general laws behind the array of particular instances, such as the Mendelian laws which manifest themselves in the bewildering variety of genetic mutations. At this stage the adolescent can consider hypotheses and figure out what should follow if they are true. He can follow the *form* of reasoning while ignoring its content, which is why the operations of this period are called *formal*. He can deal with purely hypothetical concepts such as five-dimensional space or with mathematical models such as matrices.

Men whose thinking is at the level of formal operations are

those who work out the structures of atoms, design computers, or plan the explorations of outer space. The object of their thought is the product of previous thought and may have no exemplification in reality. Einstein's theory of relativity was the product of high-level formal operations, as was the work of astronomers who deduced that there must be another planet in our system and subsequently discovered Pluto. The characteristics of this period will be described further in Chapter 8.

5

---

conservation

Conservation is the ability to realize that certain attributes of an object are constant, even though it changes in appearance. Through Piaget's conservation experiments, which are probably his most famous, he demonstrates the stages of cognition as it develops from early childhood through adolescence. Piaget takes two balls of soft clay, making sure that the child agrees that they are equal. He rolls one out into a fat sausage and asks whether the amount of clay is still the same. The child younger than about seven years of age thinks that the sausage contains more clay because it is longer. His perception is immediate, egocentric, and limited to the present. He centers his attention on a single, striking feature of the clay—its extended length—and cannot take into account the fact that while the sausage is longer, it is also thinner. If the clay is rolled back into a ball, the child will once more agree that the two balls are equal. But if one of the balls is again rolled into a sausage, the child will again insist that it is bigger. He does not yet comprehend that matter is conserved regardless of changes in form. Piaget says he has not acquired *reversibility*, the ability to follow a series of size transformations and then reverse direction and think back to when the same piece of clay was a round ball. This would require that the underlying constancy of matter be preserved in thought, and the young child is not yet capable of operating in thought independently of what he sees before him. He cannot get away from the compelling characteristic of the stimulus—its length—and see that the length is compensated for by the lesser thickness, and that therefore the amount of clay in the sausage is the same as in the ball.

Piaget uses the word *operations* to refer to actions in thought, or mental operations as opposed to physical actions. A child who cannot escape from the compelling aspects of the immediate concrete stimulus and think about what it looked like previously is said to be in the *preoperational* or prethought period. This is roughly the preschool period as well. It follows the sensory-motor period of infancy and lasts until the child is about seven, the traditional "age of reason." It is followed by the period of *concrete operations*, in which the child is capable of operating in thought upon concrete objects. Piaget demonstrates, through his conservation experiments, the various changes that occur in the child's thinking as he matures.

We have already seen how the preoperational child responds to the immediate appearance of two equal amounts of clay when one is rolled into a sausage shape. But toward the end of the preoperational period the child enters a transitional stage in which he becomes more flexible and mobile in his thinking. He may notice that the sausage is not nearly as thick as the round ball of clay, in which case he will say it contains less clay than the ball. Or he may hesitate between length and width and begin to see that the sausage is also very skinny to compensate for its length. The child is in a state of disequilibrium, pulled back and forth between various aspects of the stimulus. If the sausage is made very short and fat, he may at first say there is no difference between it and the ball, but as it is rolled out thinner and thinner he succumbs to the perceptual illusion of the increased length and says it is really bigger than the ball. Eventually he will realize that the dimensions are related, that when the sausage is shorter it is also thicker. When he can consistently and with certainty see that all changes in length are compensated for by inverse changes in width, the child has passed into the period of concrete operations. He may even wonder why you are asking him such stupid and obvious questions! He has achieved understanding of the constancy of attributes in changing objects just as he achieved understanding of the constancy of objects in changing settings during the sensory-motor period.

Piaget goes on to show that concepts of conservation are not all achieved at the same time. First the child acquires the concept of conservation of substance. He will agree that the amount of clay in each piece is the same regardless of shape. But he still does not realize that they weigh the same or have the same volume. Repeated experiments have shown that the concept of conservation of weight during changes in form comes later, and that the conservation of volume, as measured by the displacement of water, is not acquired until age eleven or twelve. Again we see here the upward spiraling of cognitive development, repeated in more complex forms at different levels. Several investigators, most notably Norwegian psychologist Jan Smedslund,[1] have repeated Piaget's experiments with approximately the same results. These three con-

cepts of conservation—first substance, then weight, then
volume—appear in that sequence despite experimental efforts
to accelerate or change their acquisition through external
reinforcement.

Piaget uses the evidence of these experiments as arguments
for the development of cognitive structures through maturation.
Experience with handling, measuring, pouring, is obviously of
basic importance in the development of such structures. But
no amount of experience or experimenting, says Piaget, can
give a child the notion of the amount of substance.

This conservation of substance is simply a logical necessity. The
child now understands that when there is a transformation you
come back to the point of departure and once again have the ball.
He knows that something is conserved but he doesn't know what. It
is not yet the weight, it is not yet the volume; it is simply a logical
form . . . a logical necessity. There, it seems to me, is an example
of progress in knowledge, a logical necessity for something to be
conserved even though no experience can have led to this notion.[2]

Piaget would never deny the role of experience in a child's
cognitive development. Even a reflex, he says, must be used in
order to adapt itself to external reality. All children suck, but
some adapt to breasts and some to bottles.

"Only practice will lead to normal functioning. That is the
first aspect of accommodation: contact with the object modifies,
in a way, the activity of the reflex, and even if this activity
were oriented hereditarily to such contact the latter is no less
necessary to the consolidation of the former. This is how certain instincts are lost or certain reflexes cease to function
normally, due to the lack of a suitable environment."[3] In other
words, even though a baby is born with a sucking reflex, he
needs something to suck or he may gradually lose his sucking
ability.

Here Piaget seems to be supporting the theory of critical

periods, the notion that certain aspects of development must receive practice at the time the organism is ready to perform them or that particular ability will not develop. For example, a child who is never talked to or encouraged to respond between the years of one and four when his speech mechanisms are developing, may have great difficulty learning to speak later on. Piaget, in like manner, emphasizes the role of maturation in cognitive development. The succession of stages which he describes is constant, even though the chronological ages at which they appear may differ from child to child and from one society to another. He cites the results of Monique Laurendeau and Adrien Pinard, Canadian psychologists who carried out many of Piaget's experiments and found the same stages among children in Montreal. But when they redid the study in Martinique, they found a delay of about four years in achieving the different stages. Piaget explains this as being due to a very relaxed, simple, nonchallenging tropical civilization. He himself found a systematic delay of two years among children in the Swiss countryside, as compared to Geneva children.

Many experimenters have repeated Piaget's conservation experiments in an effort to see whether children could not be taught to achieve these *logical structures* sooner. Piaget admits that with external reinforcement children might learn to give the right answers in limited experiments. But he implies it is a waste of time, as meaningless as teaching a dog to walk on his hind legs. This is not true learning in his view; it is an artificial, verbally acquired, "deformed" response, a rote memorization of responses to a specific situation only. It is neither stable nor permanent; children will revert quickly to the usual errors, nor can they generalize to similar situations. The logical structure can be acquired only through internal equilibrium, Piaget insists. Until a child is around seven he is not capable of grasping the notion of conservation because he does not have the logical structures, the mental organization for dealing with them. In this Piaget disagrees with some Americans, notably psychologist Jerome Bruner of Harvard, who believes that any subject can be taught at any age if it is presented in an appropriate form. He chuckles quietly over the urgency of educators in this country who are always trying to speed up the stages of cognitive development. He has been asked so often whether this could be done that he calls it "the American question." He does, however, admit that the child who has a good mental inheritance and an environment which encourages creative experimentation may achieve logical structures at an earlier age. In this sense, as Elkind points out, "Piaget's is both a nature *and* a nurture theory."[4]

There are many other kinds of experiments described by Piaget to show how fundamental the concept of conservation is. One might measure one cup of orange juice into a tall thin glass and another cup into a shallow glass bowl, and note the different cognitive levels of response. Most children younger than seven will say the glass holds more because the level of juice in it is higher, although some children may choose the bowl because it is wider. Then there will be a period of disequilibrium, and finally, when the concept of conservation is achieved, the children will see that both receptacles hold the same amount of juice. It is interesting to try these experiments with children and listen to their comments, although it should be noted that the children must be tested separately or they will influence each other's thinking. A student of mine once reported that her little brother refused to drink his milk one day because it didn't come up to the top of the glass. His mother, who had no more milk in the house, did her best to persuade him to drink what he had, with no success. Then the student, mindful of her studies of Piaget, simply poured the milk into a smaller glass so that it came to the top. "Now I'll have enough," said her little brother, and drank his milk happily.

Other Piagetian experiments demonstrate the development of the conservation of number. One might have a child count out the same number of beads twice, dropping them first into

Figure 2

a tall narrow jar and then into a shallow container. Even though he himself put the same number of beads into each container, the young child will respond to the perceptual illusion created by the shape of the container. The conservation of number is also illustrated by presenting two equal rows of buttons, and then spreading out one row or arranging it in two rows instead of one. The preoperational child will say that the double row or the spread-out row contains more buttons. If, instead of being spread out, the buttons in one of the original rows are pushed close together, the child will say that the shorter row contains fewer buttons. The child who is just entering the concrete operational phase will count the buttons each time and then say the number is the same. The child of ten or eleven will count only once and then assert the constancy of the original number so long as no buttons are added or taken away.

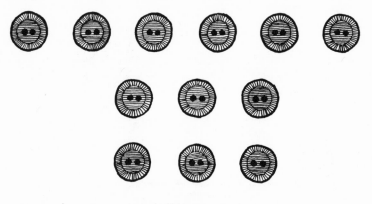

Figure 3

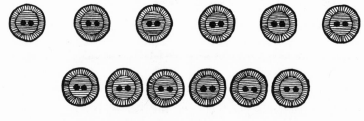

Another experiment demonstrating the conservation of length uses two identical sticks. When they are laid parallel to each other, the child will state that they are of equal length. But when one is moved ahead of the other, the preoperational child will maintain it is longer. "It's bigger because you pushed it," one of Piaget's children told him. "That [unmoved]

one is smaller because it doesn't touch there," said a five-year-old, pointing to the protruding end of the stick which had been moved. But a seven-year-old responded sagely, "They're still the same, they can't grow. . . . They're always the same length and they'll always stay the same."[5]

The results are similar when two lines of equal length are drawn on a blackboard. The one which extends farthest to the right is seen as longer. If an undulating line is drawn, covering

Figure 4

the same horizontal distance as a straight line, the young child will say it is the same length as the straight line. But the child who has achieved the concept of conservation will point out that "if you count the ups and downs the wavy line is much longer." These are some of the many ingenious ways in which Piaget demonstrates the development of conservation. Once a child has firmly acquired the logical structure, the mental understanding of the problem, he cannot be fooled by the external physical appearance of objects. Piaget quotes one little boy who said, "Once you know, you know for always."[6]

6

the preoperational child

The genius of Piaget is never more apparent than in his analysis of the little child's way of thinking. He is the rare psychologist who really listens to children and tries to understand not only what they are saying but why they are saying it. When he did not understand the "why" questions of the preschool children at the Maison des Petits in Geneva, he recorded all the questions asked by two little boys of six: "Why are there waves only at the edge of the lake?" "Why do butterflies die so soon?" "Why are you going away?" "Why can you see lightning better at night?"[1]

Then Piaget put these questions to 600 other children, mostly boys from four to nine. Among other things, he discovered that they believed everything has a reason and a purpose. When a little boy asked why there were two mountains above Geneva, the answer he wanted was that the big one was for big people to climb, and the little one was for children. When he asked why a marble was rolling down a hill, he was not satisfied with an explanation about an inclined plane; he wanted to know whether the marble "knows you are down there."

In other words, in the preoperational period the child with his needs and purposes is still the "raison d'être" of the universe; everything is made for man and children according to an established and wise plan with the human being at its center. We have seen how the baby, during the sensory-motor period, gives up his egocentric point of view on the physical level as he becomes aware of the permanence of objects and people around him. On the mental level, however, it is a long time before he relinquishes his egocentrism. This is clearly revealed in the child's assumption that the world was created for him. It permeates his thinking in many other ways as well—ways that Piaget uncovered by his open-ended way of questioning his young subjects. His findings are recorded in his five early books (see Appendix B), which are still his best known. In them a picture emerges of how the world appears to children which is quite different from how it appears to us, or how we usually assume (if we think about it at all) that it appears to them. Piaget's descriptions of children at play or in conversation are charming as well as penetrating. One pictures the young psychologist, down on his knees in the dirt playing marbles with a little Swiss boy, in order to study the morality implicit in the rules of the game.

"You must show me how to play," he says. "When I was little I used to play a lot, but now I've quite forgotten how to. I'd like to play again. Let's play together. You teach me the rules and I'll play with you."[2]

Then come the questions. Have people always played as

they do today? Where do rules come from? Who makes them up? Could you make up your own private rules? What does it mean to play "fair"? And so on, through the problems of punishment to the development of the idea of justice. It is his sensitivity to the child's point of view, his willingness to accept rather than instruct him, which makes Piaget's approach so fascinating and at the same time so revolutionary. As he remarks plaintively, "It is so hard not to talk too much when questioning a child, especially for a pedagogue."[3]

Piaget's results, first published in the early 1920's, shocked and astounded many readers. Dr. Wayne Dennis, a well-known American psychologist, was unconvinced. He proceeded to put some of Piaget's questions to his own little daughter of almost three.[4] To his surprise, the child showed many of the characteristics of preoperational thought described by Piaget. Today, fifty years and many follow-up studies later, Piaget's ideas have been pretty much corroborated. Consequently, they have had a tremendous impact on our understanding of children and our ways of approaching them.

The egocentrism of the young child leads him to assume that everyone thinks as he does, and that the whole world shares his feelings and desires. This sense of oneness with the world leads naturally to the child's assumption of magic omnipotence. The world not only is created for him; he can control it. The sun and the moon must follow him when he goes for a walk, or he can make the rain come by dancing around in circles.

When J. was 5;6(11) I overheard a conversation between her and L. in bed. L. was afraid of the dark and J. was reassuring her. L. then asked: "Where does the dark come from?—*From water, because when it's daylight, the night goes into the lake.*" But at 5;6(22) I heard J. alone in the garden saying: "*I'm making the daylight come up, I'm making it come up* (making a gesture of raising something from the ground). *Now I'm making it go away* (gesture of pushing something away) *and now the night's coming. I make the night come up when I go to the edge of the lake: the man* (walking outside the garden) *still has a bit on his coat. I'm making the light come up.*" After this, she amused herself the rest of the day in "*making light*" with a stick (making the gesture of pulling it towards her and throwing it away).[5]

Here there is obvious similarity to the magic rituals of primitive tribes. Such rituals are recorded in the rhymes of childhood, such as "Rain, rain, go away," or "Step on a crack, you'll break your mother's back." The implication is that the child by his behavior or incantations can control the forces of nature. Vestiges of such childish magic are familiar to many of us who snap our fingers to make the red light change or carry an umbrella "to make sure it won't rain."

Another manifestation of the child's egocentrism is his inability to put himself in the position of another person. This is apparent on both physical and intellectual levels. The child who has learned his own right and left sides cannot identify the same positions on a person facing him. He cannot describe how a view or a topological display appears to a person looking at it from another angle. Piaget realized this when he took his son Laurent for an automobile ride and discovered that the boy did not recognize the familiar mountain which rises behind Geneva. Seen from his own garden he knew it well; seen from a new perspective it looked different, so Laurent assumed that it was the mountain, not his point of view, which was strange.

In the same way a child has difficulty understanding another person's intellectual or emotional point of view. Elkind has suggested that it is the child's egocentrism, and not his moral perversity, which makes him continue to pester his mother when she has told him she has a headache and wants to be left alone.[6] Any parent who has tried to sleep when a youngster is playing cowboys at dawn knows the futility of expecting the "Bang-bang!" to stop, no matter how reasonable (to the parent) the request.

The egocentric point of view also shows itself at the level of children's speech. The young child cannot repeat a story in a way that is clear to the listener who does not know the plot. Most adults are familiar with the recital that goes: ". . . and then he came, and she said . . ." with never a clue as to who he and she are! The preoperational child cannot reconstruct his own reasoning, or justify his arguments, because he cannot think about them objectively or from another person's point of view. In fact, he assumes that all the world shares his thoughts and feelings and that therefore he need not explain them. It takes a good many years of interaction with others for him to outgrow this egocentric attitude.

Another characteristic of egocentric thought is known as *animism*. The child believes that the world of nature is alive, conscious, and endowed with purpose like himself. This arises because the child, being unconscious of himself, confuses himself with the universe. The sun follows the child to "show him the way"; the clouds move by themselves and chart their course. This dynamic view of the world, activated by energy and life, is like the primitive cosmologies of tribes such as the Hopi Indians, who believe every tree and every spring is inhabited by a living spirit.

> *"The sun sometimes watches us,"* says Fran (9), *"when we're looking nice he looks at us.—Do you look nice?—Yes, on Sundays, when I'm dressed like a man."*
>
> *"The moon looks at us and watches over us,"* says Ga (8½), *"when I walk, it walks; when I stand still it stands still. It copies like a parrot.—Why?—It wants to do whatever I do.—Why?— Because it's inquisitive."*[7]

Piaget observed four stages in the development of animism. Up to four or five years old, the child believes anything may be endowed with purpose and conscious activity. A ball may refuse to be thrown straight, or a "naughty" chair may be responsible for bumping him. Then a transition stage occurs in which the child experiences cognitive conflict and may reverse or contradict himself. Only objects which move, such as floating clouds or a moving car, are alive. Their movements may be determined by physical compulsion or moral necessity; for example, the clouds "know they must move because they bring rain." In the third stage, only objects which move spontaneously are alive; cars or bicycles, which move only when driven by an outside agent, are not. The last stage, in which only plants and animals are considered alive, does not come until about eleven or twelve.

Roger Russell and Wayne Dennis[8] standardized Piaget's questions on animism by making up a list of twenty objects. The first five objects, including some chipped and broken ones, were actually shown to each child. These psychologists found that children, even in the earliest stage, would not attribute life to a broken button or a chipped dish. The instructions for this interview follow along with answers obtained from a five-year-old girl by one of my students.

Instructions: We are going to play a game. I am going to ask you some questions and we will see how many you can answer. You know what it means to be alive? A cat is alive, isn't it? Tell me something else that's alive. Why? How do you know it's (not) alive? (Repeat this after each object on the list.) Show child the first five objects if possible.

1. Stone—Alive, because it moves.
2. Pencil—Alive, because it writes.
3. Button (broken)—If it's broken, it's no use. It's dead.
4. Watch—It's alive if it tells time, but it's dead if it can't tell time.
5. Dish (chipped)—It's just as dead as a broken button.

6. Candle—Only if it is lit. (What would happen if the light went out, and then came on again?) It would die, then it would come back to life.
7. Bicycle—Alive, because it runs.
8. Chair—Alive, because people sit on it.
9. River—Alive when people go in it.
10. Clouds—Alive, because they're moving all the time.
11. Tree—Alive, because it's waving and growing.
12. Sun—It's always alive, because God helps it.
13. Wind—Alive, because it blows. But when it does not blow, it's not dead; it's just asleep.
14. Automobile—Alive, because it runs.
15. Bird—Alive, because it flies. When they are shot, birds are dead.
16. Fire—Alive, because it goes.
17. Dog—Alive, because it walks.
18. Grass—Alive, because it grows.
19. Bug—Yes, alive, because it runs.
20. Flower—Alive, because people water it a lot.

To this little girl, an object's functioning is very important. Chairs and rivers are alive only when being used by people, another illustration of the egocentric attitude discussed earlier. She is obviously approaching Stage II, however, because some objects (watch, candle) are alive only when they are moving.

Closely related to animism is *artificialism*, the tendency of the child to believe that human beings created natural phenomena. Piaget's little daughter, seeing the clouds of smoke rising from her father's pipe, assumed that Papa was responsible for the clouds in the sky and the mists around the mountaintops of Switzerland.

Piaget's first awareness of this belief came from listening to questions which suggested it. "Who made the sun?" "Who is it puts the stars in the sky at night?" "What makes the moon shine?" Putting the same questions back to the children, he learned that the sun and the moon were made by men, from a flame or a match—or by God, who closely resembled a man. "God lit [the sun] with wood and coal." "Some men made it into a big ball . . . then afterwards they told it to go up in the air." "People took little stones and made them into little stars." The waning moon disappears because "it is hidden in heaven by God." Children in Geneva believe that the lake there was dug by men to serve the city after it had already been built. Such thinking is not so different from the anthropocentric view of the world expressed in the Old Testament, in which God created heaven and earth and set the moon and stars in the sky.

Further expressing his egocentrism, the young child regards his own perspective as immediately objective and absolute. To him all things are equally real—words, pictures, dreams, or feelings. Piaget calls this attitude *realism*—the child ignores the fact that his is only one point of view, and thinks that what is real for him must exist objectively. Names, for example, are real and exist as part of the thing named. The young child cannot conceive that he could have been given another name. One is reminded of the beliefs of primitive people in the magic of names and the power they give to one who knows them, exemplified in the story of Rumpelstiltskin.

As the child grows older he begins to realize that names are not an intrinsic part of the object named, but come from somewhere. In transitional stages he will say that the name of the sun is in the sky, or floating in the air, rather than that it is in the sun (i.e., part of it). Or, as in the following example, he may say the moon was given its name by God.

Stei (5½): "Have you a name?—*Yes, André.*—And that?— *A box.*—And that?—*A pen*, etc.—What are names for?—*They are what you can see when you look at things* (Stei thus believes that one has only to look at a thing to 'see' its name)—Why have you got a name?—*So as to know what I'm called.*—Then what are names for?—*To know what things are called.*—How did the sun get its name in the beginning?—*I don't know.*—What do you think?—*Because the sun made the name, the sun gave it in the beginning and so the sun is called sun.*—And how did you get your name?—*We have to be christened.*—Who christened you?—*The clergyman.*—And did you take your name?—*The clergyman makes it for us.*—How did the moon get its name?—*The moon? The moon is called the moon.*—How did it start being called moon?—*God called it that in the beginning.*—How did the clouds start being called clouds?—*God started them by making them.*—But are the clouds' names the same thing as the clouds?—*Yes, the same thing.*"[9]

The writer once questioned a little girl whose parents were Japanese. The child had been born in this country but had always heard of Japan as a faraway, mythical source of her family's beginnings. When asked where the sun got its name, she replied, "From Japan." This child's older cousin had recently gone back to Japan, so the little girl was asked where her cousin was, and then where her cousin's name was. To the second question she replied, "At the airport"—the last place where she had seen her cousin! Another child, who realized that her name was not a part of her body, said it was "in her pocket." It is not until around six or seven that children realize that names are only verbal labels existing in the minds of the people who use them.

Piaget made an interesting study of realism in children's dreams and found that young children are quite convinced that their dreams are real. At the earliest stage children, when asked where their dreams come from, give them an external origin. Dreams come "from the night," "from the sky," or "from God." Some children believe that it is the people they dream of who cause the dream. This is probably related to the emotional aspect of dreams—they come "because we've done something we ought not to" or because "I saw a man who frightened me in the day and I dreamed of it at night." To the question, "While you dream, where is the dream?" young children answer "in the room," "against the wall," or "in the bed."

Zeng (6): "Where do dreams come from?—*They come from the night.*—How?—*I don't know.*—What do you mean by 'they come from the night'?—*The night makes them.*—Does the dream come by itself?—*No.*—What makes it?—*The night.*—Where is the dream?—*It's made in the room.*—Where does the dream come from?—*From the sky.*—Is the dream made in the sky?—*No.*—Where is it made?—*In the room.*"[10]

Thus the dream is caused externally and appears externally. It is only when children know that their dreams originate internally and exist internally, although they *appear* to be externalized, that the stage of objective reality is achieved. In between exist various degrees of confusion as to how the dream "comes out" as soon as one is asleep, so that its origin is internal but its existence is external. The child in this transition stage confuses *being* with *seeming;* the dream must be outside because "you can't see what is inside the head!" A further source of confusion is that the child remembers seeing himself in the dream but knows he was in bed at the time he dreamed. One little boy of eight drew a picture for Piaget showing himself in his nightshirt, standing in front of the devil, complete with horns, who was about to boil him. Over at the side was the same little boy lying in bed, watching the proceedings![11] This was a very clear example of child realism.

The reasoning of the preoperational child is based not on logic but on contiguity. Objects and events that occur together are assumed to have a causal relationship. The road makes the bicycle go; by creating a shadow one can cause the night to come. The thunder makes it rain, and honking the horn makes the car go. How many people around New York thought they had personally caused the 1965 blackout by plugging in a cord or turning on an appliance? Closely related to this kind of reasoning is the formation of associations between things without any logical connection, just because, to the child, they seem to "go together." Piaget quotes a little boy who said, "The moon doesn't fall down because there is no sun because it is very high up." These are three separate facts the child has observed about the moon, none of which have any relation to one another. One sometimes observes adults whose thinking is based on egocentric thinking rather than on logic. Gracie Allen and Lucille Ball have both amused millions with this sort of cockeyed *non sequitur*.

We have already considered briefly the importance of the young child's make-believe play. Piaget feels that this represents a step in the development of thought. The child who is using his blocks as the *symbolic representation* of a train is assimilating all the characteristics of trains he has seen—they move, they go "choo-choo," they are strung out along the track. To him the blocks *are* a train, and woe betide anyone who kicks them off the track! The child's egocentrism prevents him from realizing that his precious train is only a row of blocks to his harassed mother, who would like to have a tidy living room.

Later, the child may be satisfied with only a verbal symbol; the word "train" which will become for him the mental representation of all the attributes of a train. Thus the development of "make-believe" play and language represents intermediate steps between sensory-motor activities and the later stages of thought alone. As such, they are both colored by the child's egocentric thinking.

In the realm of language we have already spoken of the child's assumption that the adult knows what is on his mind without his having explained it. Many of the "cute sayings" of the little child, the original words and expressions he coins, are part of his own private, egocentric language. I puzzled for some time, listening to a little boy talk about his "mocha troll" horse, before realizing that he meant "remote control"! It takes a long time before words acquire socialized meanings; the egocentrism of the child makes it difficult for him to realize that what *he* means by his private language is not necessarily what others may mean. This is why childhood in the human species is such an extended period. It is only gradually that equilibrium can be established between assimilation and accommodation, so that a stable symbolic representation is established to which a verbal symbol can be attached. Like many another embarrassed father, Piaget heard his little girl saying "Daddy" to all sorts of strange men before she really knew what the word meant.

Listening to young children talk to each other, Piaget noted that "they speak as though they were talking to themselves," even though they think they are listening to each other. Piaget calls this *collective monologue* rather than a real exchange of ideas. At the preschool level the children are talking alongside each other, just as they play alongside each other, rather than cooperatively. They also spend a good deal of time talking to themselves, and these private conversations can be most revealing to the parent who listens with a sensitive ear.

Thus, during the preoperational period the child reveals his egocentrism in his play and conversation, in his questions, beliefs, and expectations. It is a long period, and one in which the child has to relearn on a conceptual level much of what he has already mastered at the sensory-motor level. In infancy the child learned that objects continued to exist even when they were out of sight. In early childhood he learns that objects are the same even when they appear in different forms. The three-year-old may not recognize his grandmother in a new out-fit or a familiar object in a new setting. Piaget describes how Jacqueline, at 2;7, seeing Lucienne in a new bathing suit and cap, asked, "What's the baby's name?" When her mother ex-plained that it was a new bathing suit, Jacqueline pointed right at Lucienne's face and said, "But what's the name of *that?*" As soon as Lucienne had changed her clothes, Jacqueline ex-claimed, "It's Lucienne again!" as if Lucienne "had changed her identity in changing her clothes."[12]

During this period, the child must develop *perceptual con-stancy*, so that he recognizes that objects are the same even when seen in differing surroundings (see Chapter 15). This achievement will then pave the way for the next logical struc-ture, which is the conservation of matter. As we have previously seen, the child who has reached this level realizes that matter or quantity is constant, however much it is changed in form. A cup of milk is a cup, regardless of the shape of the glass it is in.

A major achievement of this period is the ability to deal with symbols. We have already seen how Lucienne, at the end of the sensory-motor period, was able to use her mouth to represent a matchbox. During early childhood children are learning various kinds of symbolic representation. Learning to talk represents a great forward step in communication and socializa-tion. As a child is able to ask questions and express his magical, distorted ideas, they become corrected by adults through the use of language. The ability to draw pictures and the invention of "make-believe" games also represent symbolic processes. The origin and development of these processes will be taken up at length later (see Chapters 11 and 12).

Piaget divides the preoperational period into two parts. The

years from two to four he calls the stage of *preconcepts*. By this
he refers to the young child's first fuzzy attempts at generalization. The child hasn't had enough experience to understand the
relation between representatives of a class and the class itself.
In the following excerpt, Jacqueline distinguishes between bees
and bumblebees, but doesn't differentiate between insects and
animals. Moreover, one slug is just like the next to her, so she
thinks it's the same one, rather than another representative of
the same species.

Observation 107. J. at 2;6(3) : *"That's not a bee, it's a bumble-*
bee. Is it an animal?" But also at about 2;6 she used the term *the*
slug for the slugs we went to see every morning along a certain
road. At 2;7(2) she cried: *"There it is!"* on seeing one, and when
we saw another ten yards further on she said: *"There's the slug*
again." I answered: "But isn't it another one?" J. then went back
to see the first one. "Is it the same one?—*Yes.*—Another slug?—
Yes.—Another or the same?" The question obviously had no
meaning for J.

At 3;3(0) J. was playing with a red insect, which disappeared.
A quarter of an hour later when we were out for a walk we tried
to look at a lizard, which darted away. Ten minutes afterwards we
found another red insect. *"It's the red animal again.*—Do you
think so?—*Where's the lizard then?"*[13]

The growth of the ability to think in terms of images, then
symbols, and then concepts will be discussed in greater detail
in Chapter 12. The second stage of preoperational thought,
which Piaget calls the *intuitive* stage, will also be clarified.
Piaget uses the term *intuitive*, and sometimes *perceptual*, to
describe the thought of this later phase, because the child is
feeling his way toward logical thinking but is constantly deceived by the perceptual appearance of things, as we noted in
the conservation experiments. In the years between four and
seven the child is able to cope very well with the physical world
around him, on the basis of sensory-motor activities and per-

ceptual adaptations. His thought life, however, is still un-adapted to the reality of the world. It is egocentric, illogical, and dramatically different from that of adults. Parents tend to see their children as reflections of themselves—but Piaget has led us through this looking-glass into the magic, delightful, distorted world of childhood.

7

concrete operations

Piaget uses the term *operations* for activities of the mind, as opposed to the bodily activities of the sensory-motor period. The preoperational child can form mental pictures or symbolic representations, as evidenced by his drawings, his make-believe play, and his use of language. However, he functions not logically but intuitively, depending on immediate perception and direct experience. In the experiment with the clay balls, for example, the reasoning of the preoperational child is: I perceive them to be different; therefore, they must be different. The child who is operating logically reasons: They were the same to begin with, so they must be the same now, even though they look different.

Thus the operational child is freed from the pull of immediate perception. He is also able to range forward and back-

ward in space and time on the mental level. This speeds up
the thinking process immeasurably and gives it much greater
mobility and freedom. The preoperational child who loses a
toy will search in every room where he has been; the operational child can sit still and think back over where he has been
until he can logically decide where he probably left it. This
process demonstrates the quality of reversibility, which characterizes the thinking of the child of six or seven who has
reached the period of concrete operations. In spite of his new
freedom, however, he is capable only of thought about concrete,
existing objects and people. The realm of hypothetical thought,
dealing with theories and propositions, will not be attainable
until his adolescent years.

In order to describe the intellectual structures which develop
in the school-age child, Piaget turned to the language of logic
and mathematics. In mathematics, a *group* is a set of elements
whose relations with each other have the properties of combinativity, associativity, identity, and reversibility. These are
terms familiar to those now being exposed to the "new math"
in schools.

Combinativity (or *composition*) means that any two groups
may be combined into one inclusive group: $2 + 2 = 4$, boys
and girls are children, $A + A' = B$, $B + B' = C$.

Associativity refers to the fact that the sum of a series is
independent of its order. Two rows of three buttons or three
rows of two buttons both make a total of six buttons. (Piaget's
anecdote about the little boy arranging pebbles in his garden
illustrates this principle.)

Identity requires that one of the elements of a group be
such that combining it with any other element leaves that
element unchanged. In addition, the identity element is 0;
adding 0 to any number leaves it unchanged. In multiplication,
1 is the identity element; multiplying any number by 1 leaves
it unchanged.

Reversibility means that each element in the set has an opposite which, combined with it, reverses the operation to its starting point. There are two kinds of reversibility: one produces a negation of the previous operation (i.e., $2 + 2 = 4$, so $4 - 2 = 2$), whereas the other simply produces its reciprocal, or opposite (i.e., if A is less than B, B must be greater than A).

At the stage of concrete operations, Piaget observed, most structures of thought do not satisfy these requirements for a mathematical group. In fact, he described only two such groups, one involving addition, and the other multiplication, which he found in the child's arithmetical operations. However, he did note a number of organized structures of thought which, though they do not possess mathematical properties, are reversible and logically organized in the sense that every element is related to every other one. Piaget called these structures logical *groupings* (translated from the French *groupements*). They include the logic of classes and the logic of relations. The

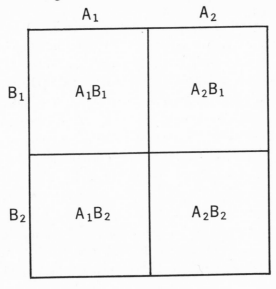

Figure 5

former refers to operations of class inclusion, which require that a child be able to manipulate part-whole relationships within a set of categories. Classes may be added to form a larger class; i.e., dogs plus cats are animals, $A + A' = B$. They may also be multiplied; multiplication in logic simply requires that every element be combined with every other. Multiplying objects or properties on the basis of two criteria would produce the double-entry tables familiar to most people. For example, if we multiply to get all possible combinations of dogs (A_1) and cats (A_2), brown ones (B_1) and black ones (B_2), we would come out with brown dogs, brown cats, black dogs, and black cats $(A_1B_1, A_1B_2, B_2A_1, B_2A_2)$.

Logically, more than two classes could be multiplied as well, and Piaget includes such a grouping in order to make his classifications logically consistent. There is no empirical research to indicate that children understand or think in terms of such a complicated relationship, however, so we will turn from the addition and multiplication of classes to the logic of relations.

This term refers to serial ordering operations by which children can arrange things in increasing or decreasing order. If A is greater than B, $(A > B)$ and B is greater than C $(B > C)$ then A is greater than C $(A > C)$. Such relationships are described as asymmetric because there is no indication that the relationship between them is consistent; we do not know by how much A is greater than B. Relationships can be asymmetric or symmetric, as in family relationships in which if X is the brother of Y, and Y is the cousin of Z, then X is the cousin of Z. In either case they can be added and multiplied; again, multiplication may be on the basis of two relationships, or of more. Piaget's explanation of the eight possible logical groupings is very long, very detailed, and very difficult to follow except for the trained mathematician or logician. Those who share his passion for orderly classification and algebraic formulation are referred to Flavell[1] or Baldwin,[2] as well as to Inhelder and Piaget's books[3] on the growth of logical thinking. Suffice it to say that the eighth grouping, called "Co-univocal multiplication of relations," contains equations such as this:

$$(A \xleftrightarrow{a'} \downarrow {}^{b}B) \times (B \xleftrightarrow{o'} \downarrow {}^{a}C) = A \xleftrightarrow{a'} \downarrow {}^{c}C.$$

To the initiated, this represents a relationship such as the following: if A is first cousin to the grandfather of B, and B is the brother of the father of C, it follows that A is first cousin to the great-grandfather of C.[4]

Rather than attempt to discuss each of these logical groupings, we will consider only certain ones for which Piaget devised experiments, and which can be clearly shown to exist in the organization of children's thought.

A very simple fundamental grouping is concerned with the relationship of identity or equivalence. If $A = B$, and $B = C$, then $A = C$. As an example of this, Piaget asked a group of boys if they had brothers. One little boy named Paul said yes, he had a brother named Etienne. Asked if Etienne had a brother, the boy said he did not. His limited point of view prevented him from realizing that he bore the same relationship to Etienne as Etienne did to him. He did not put himself in the picture, whereas an older child would realize logically that he must be Etienne's brother if Etienne was his. For Piaget, this represented a preliminary stage of concrete operations.

The first important grouping is called *the additive composition of classes*. It describes the organization among a set of nested classes in which each one is included in the next larger one, like a set of mixing bowls. This kind of grouping applies to many relationships. Boys and girls are children; children and adults are people; people and nonhuman mammals are

mammals. This grouping is expressed algebraically as A + A′
= B, B + B′ = C, C + C′ = D, and so on. The relationships
can be reversed; B − A′ = A, or children, excluding girls, are
boys. To demonstrate children's grasp of this sort of hierarchical classification, Piaget gave them objects which could be
sorted into classes on the basis of different characteristics.

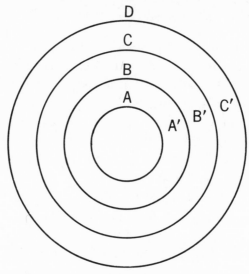

Figure 6

This sort of experiment is the backbone of all psychological
research on concept formation; in fact there is an intelligence
test based on exactly this kind of object sorting (Hanfmann-
Kasinin Concept Formation Test).

   In one experiment in this series, Piaget and his co-worker
Inhelder presented their subjects with a variety of geometric
figures, some made of wood and some of plastic. Moreover,
objects of the same shape came in different colors; there were
red and blue squares as well as circles. The children were asked
to put together the objects that were alike. They might group
them on the basis of shape, or color, or material, or even
angularity as opposed to roundness.

The results showed that the youngest children tended to form what Piaget called "graphic collections." The objects were sorted on some basis of similarity, but the bases tended to change as a child proceeded. For example, he might make a row of four squares, the last two of which were red. Then, as if the redness took precedence over the shape, he might add red circles or red triangles. Some children made simple designs, others more complex mosaics; in other words, the sorting was based not on logical classes but on perceptual attributes.

Jos (3;1) first places six semi-circles (two blue, two yellow, one red and one blue) in a line. Then she puts a yellow triangle on a blue square, and then a red square between two blue triangles with all three touching. She goes on to make a row of almost all the squares and triangles (touching one another still, but the shapes and colors taken haphazard). She now places a triangle and three squares in a line, and while doing so she decides that it is a house: she continues by adding a square below the three others. The last response therefore belongs to the category of "complex objects" (see Fig. 7).[5]

Figure 7

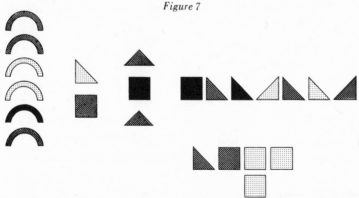

Inhelder and Piaget, *The Early Growth of Logic in the Child*, p. 21.

After a period of arranging on the basis of one or another property, such as color, the most highly developed classification emerged among the children of seven or eight. This included subdivisions based on the same criteria; for example, all squares in one group and all triangles in another, and both of these separated from the curvilinear group containing circles, half-circles and rings.

Rob (8;2), given the materials, starts with four classes: (A) the circles, semi-circles, and sectors, (B) the triangles, (C) the squares, and (D) the rings. Then he unites B and C, saying, "All the squares and triangles," but he keeps them separate in one box, and then he puts together A and D, saying, "All the rounds," which are also subdivided according to variety.[6]

A similar way of testing children's understanding of the relationship of nested classes was to lay before each child a row of counters that included red and blue squares and blue circles but no red circles. The child was then asked, "Are all the squares red?" "Are all the circles blue?" To the latter question, a four- or five-year-old would typically answer, "No, because there is a blue square." In other words, he was responding to the blueness rather than the circleness and answering the question as if it had been, "Are all the blue ones circles?" Some children also seemed not to understand the terms "all" and "some"; "all" to them meant a lot rather than only two or three. One five-year-old, who was shown three red squares, two blue squares, and two blue circles, was asked if all the circles were blue. He replied, "No, there are only two," as if "all" had to include a larger number.

One of Piaget's favorite experiments illustrates the problems children have with classification pertaining to this part-whole relationship, which he called "the inclusion of classes." It consists of presenting children with a box containing twenty wooden beads. A few were painted white; the rest were brown. The child was asked whether the box contained more wooden beads or more brown beads. Little children would answer, "More brown ones." Piaget pointed out that the young child could not think about the whole (wooden beads) and its parts (brown and white beads) at the same time. He was still functioning on a perceptual level and had succumbed to the visual impression that there were more brown beads. The difficulty of overcoming this pervasive error is illustrated by the following excerpt.

Bis (6;8): "Are there more wooden beads or more brown beads?—*More brown ones, because there are two whites ones.*— Are the white ones made of wood?—*Yes.*—And the brown ones?— *Yes.*—Then are there more brown ones or more wooden ones? —*More brown ones.*—What color would a necklace made of the wooden beads be?—*Brown and white* (thus showing that Bis clearly understood the problem).—And what color would a necklace made with the brown beads be?—*Brown.*—Then which would be longer, the one made with the wooden beads or the one made with the brown beads?—*The one with the brown beads.*—Draw the neck-laces for me. (Bis drew a series of black rings for the necklace of brown beads, and a series of black rings plus two white rings for the necklace of wooden beads.)—Good. Now which will be longer, the one with the brown beads or the one with the wooden beads?— *The one with the brown beads.*" Thus, in spite of having clearly understood, and having correctly drawn the data of the problem, Bis was unable to solve it by including the class of brown beads in the class of wooden beads![7]

This stage was followed by an intermediate stage in which the intuitive discovery of the correct answer came through trial and error. Finally the child achieved the conceptual stage, in which he could move back and forth between the parts and the whole in his thinking and could comprehend that the whole was greater than its parts. (Brown beads + white beads = wooden beads.)

Bol (6;6): *"The wooden necklace will be longer than the brown one.—Why?—Because there are more.—But why are there more? —Because there are the white ones as well."*[8]

Inhelder and Piaget also devised experiments to point up the difficulties that children have with special kinds of classes.

For example, it was much harder to form a hierarchical classification if one class contained only one member. Even more difficult was the null class, the class with no objects in it. When children were asked to sort a series of picture cards which included some blanks, even some ten- and eleven-year-olds did not realize that the blank cards formed a class of their own. This brings to mind the problems children have in dealing with the concept of zero in arithmetic. It is only when it is presented to them in a very concrete way as a place-holder that primary children can understand zero. Many teachers utilize the empty seat in a row of children, or the empty desk being held for an absent child, to help youngsters understand this place-holding concept.

Another kind of grouping described by Piaget illustrates seriation or the addition of asymmetrical relationships. This is one in which objects can be arranged in order of size or weight or height or any other property, such that A is less than B and B is less than C, so that A is less than C ($A < B$, $B < C$, therefore $A < C$). The reverse of this, of course, is the "greater than" relationship, in which objects are arranged in ascending order, with A greater than B, etc. This reversal, as we have pointed out, is not a negation as in $B - A' = A$, but is rather a reciprocal relationship; if A is less than B, then B must be greater than A.

As one way of testing the child's ability to seriate or to arrange things in a logical series, Piaget would show a child two sticks, one of which was a little longer than the other ($A > B$). Then, hiding the longer stick A, he would show him stick B and a still shorter stick C ($B > C$). With A still hidden, he would ask whether A was longer than C. A little child could not tell without actually seeing A and C together, but an older child, operating logically, would give the correct answer. (This experiment was successful only if the difference between the sticks was not too dramatic.)

This kind of serial relationship must logically precede the numerical operation of counting. In the above experiment, there is no way of knowing whether A is longer than B to the same extent that B is longer than C. If this were so, then it would be possible to move from this grouping to a numbered system of integers because the difference between A and B and between B and C would be one measured unit. The transition from asymmetrical series to counting will be explored in Chapter 13.

One more type of grouping which will be discussed here is multiplication of relations. This is a bit simpler than the sys-

Figure 8

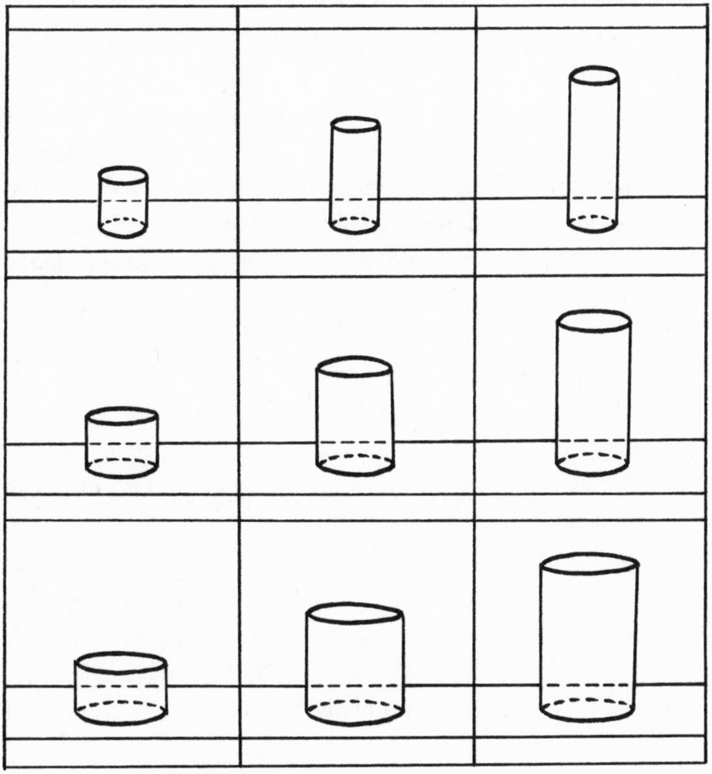

tem of family relationships previously referred to, because it deals with objects arranged in respect to only two attributes at a time, instead of several. For example, if glasses were arranged in a horizontal series by heights and in a vertical series by widths, the result would be a matrix in which height increases across the top of the matrix and width increases down the side. (See next page.) This kind of multiplication of asymmetrical relations (increasing heights multiplied by increasing widths) is what the child must deal with to understand the kinds of questions that were asked in the conservation experiments. Piaget used such a matrix with certain cells missing and asked his subjects to select what would fit in a particular cell, in terms of both horizontal and vertical dimensions. Jerome Bruner[9] has also published the results of a very similar experiment using a 3-by-3 matrix of glasses. He not only asked his subjects to replace a few glasses; he took out all the glasses and asked them to reproduce the matrix. Then he put the shortest, widest glass in the corner where the tallest, thinnest one had been, and asked them to transpose the whole matrix. As might be expected, only the oldest children in his population of three to seven years could do this successfully. Bruner found the younger children very dependent on the perceptual features of the task. They could remember where the glasses had been before and replace them in accordance with a visually perceived pattern. But only the seven-year-olds could grasp the logical organization inherent in the array of glasses and express it, like one little girl who said, "It gets fatter going one way and taller going the other."

Piaget himself studied this multiplicative relationship by asking children to put two sequences in one-to-one relationship. One such problem which younger subjects found very difficult is quoted by Flavell.[10] "There are only three knives in a store. Two of these knives have two blades; they cost eight francs and ten francs. Two of these knives have a corkscrew; they cost ten francs and twelve francs. I choose the one which has two blades and a corkscrew; how much does it cost?" Another experiment involved having each child arrange a series of dolls and then a series of canes according to size, so that each cane was paired with the right-sized doll. Piaget found that this kind of pairing could be accomplished readily by the child of about seven. However, as we shall see in the discussion of time concepts, when it came to pairing a double series in inverse order, so that as one series decreased the other increased, there was much more difficulty involved.

These, then, are some of the logical groupings which Piaget observed in the thinking of the concrete-operational child. His experiments show that from about seven years on, a child is capable of many kinds of classification and seriation. He has the ability to understand the relationships that he sees around him in actuality. What he still does not have is the ability to think of all possible kinds of relationships, whether actual or hypothetical. In discussing the period of formal operations we will describe the development of adult inferential thinking.

8

formal operations

Piaget uses the term *hypothetico-deductive thinking* to describe
the mental operations of adolescents and adults, a term which
he himself characterizes as "barbarous but clear." We have
already described such operations as *formal*, in contrast to the
concrete operations of the preadolescent. By hypothetico-deductive thinking, Piaget means thinking based upon a hypothesis
which leads to certain logical deductions. Such a hypothesis
may exist only in form (e.g., What would happen if no one
ever died?), or it may have conclusions which can be verified
in concrete reality. It was the working out of such hypotheses
that made possible the successful landing of men on the moon.
The feats of scientists who have exploded hydrogen bombs and
harnessed atomic energy are examples of the results of such
thinking. No one has ever seen atoms and electrons; yet the

dramatic developments of atomic theory are becoming part of our daily reality.

For his books on logical thinking, Piaget joined forces with Professor Bärbel Inhelder, an experimental child psychologist at the University of Geneva. She was doing research on how children and adolescents come to understand the laws of natural science at the same time that Piaget was working out his logical formulations for the structure of adolescent thought. They compared notes and realized "the striking convergence between the empirical and the analytic results."[1] Piaget's logical analysis provided the appropriate structural model for Inhelder's data on adolescent reasoning. This was the beginning of a long and scientifically fruitful relationship.

These authors have shown that the child of seven to eleven is capable of dealing with the logic of classes and relations. He understands the relationships of classes within classes; he can put objects and events in serial order. This has been called "describer-thinking," dealing with concrete facts in a real and visible world. But the adolescent is capable of inferential thinking, or what Piaget calls "second-order operations." By this he means thinking about thoughts rather than about things that exist. Not only can he deduce from hypotheses ("If . . . then . . . " propositions), but he can take account of all possible combinations of factors or relationships. He can study one variable while holding all others constant, thus carrying out complicated, multifactor experiments. To describe the integrated structures of formal operations, Piaget turned to the logic of groups and lattices. We have discussed briefly the characteristics of arithmetic groups, as opposed to groupings (see Chapter 7). But an even more sophisticated "four-group" was borrowed from the Bourbaki school of mathematicians by Piaget to express the flexibility of adolescent thought. This was a group of four transformations, known as the *INRC group*.

These letters stand for *I*dentity, *N*egation (or inverse), *R*ecip-rocal, and *C*orrelative transformations. They are best illustrated by describing an actual experiment.

To study the operational schema of equilibrium, a balance scale was set up, provided with varying weights which could be placed at different points along the crossbar. The scale was presented with equal weights on each arm, but so placed that the scale was out of equilibrium. The subjects were asked to make the arms balance. The youngest children did so by press-ing down on one arm—an extension of their own sensory-motor experience with weight as something that pushes down heavily. When asked to make the scale balance without the help of his hand, one four-and-a-half-year-old replied, "You can't!" An-other put two weights on one arm, but nothing on the other, and wondered why the scale didn't balance!

Older children began to experiment with adding weights to each side; but the idea of reversibility, of subtracting weight to reach a balance, did not emerge until around seven. Gradually, by trial and error, they groped around until they could formu-

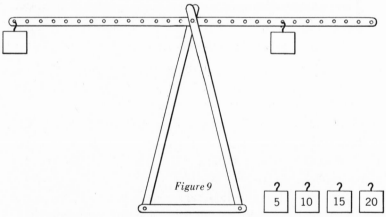

Figure 9

Taken from Inhelder & Piaget, *Growth of Logical Thinking*, p. 165.

late the law of equilibrium: "The heavier it is, the closer to the middle."

Sam (13;8) discovers immediately that the horizontal distance is inversely related to weight. "How do you explain that? *You need more force to raise weights placed at the extremes than when it's closer to the center . . . because it has to cover a greater distance.* How do you know? *If one weight on the balance is three times the other, you put it a third of the way out because the distance* (upward) *it goes is three times less.* But once you referred to the distance (horizontal gesture) and once to the path covered? *Oh, that depends on whether you have to calculate it or whether you really understand it. If you want to calculate, it's best to consider it horizontally; if you want to understand it, vertically is better. For the light one* (at the extremity) *it changes more quickly, for the heavy one less quickly.*"[2]

Here we see how the INRC group structure expresses the proportional schema. If a weight is placed on one of the arms, thus destroying the equilibrium of the scale, the balance can be restored by simply taking off the weight (negation). Or an equal weight can be added at an equal distance on the other arm (reciprocal). Third, a heavier weight can be added at a distance closer to the center, or a lighter one farther away (correlation). Last, all the weights can be removed, returning the scale to its original equilibrium (identity).

This is a very much simplified explanation of a mathematical expression which includes all possible relationships of the weights and the distances to each other. Those who understand the language of symbolic logic are referred to Chapter 11 of Inhelder and Piaget's *The Growth of Logical Thinking.* Flavell[3] and Baldwin[4] also give shortened explanations of the logic of groups and lattices.

The lattice, in mathematics, is a more sophisticated structure than the double-entry matrix which we discussed as characteristic of concrete operations. Instead of considering just black dogs, black cats, brown dogs, and brown cats, as in our earlier example, it would also include such combinations as black and brown dogs and black cats, or brown dogs and cats but no black ones. The lattice is a mathematical model which is composed of the sixteen possible combinations of four binary propositions, ranging from none of them (the null class) to all four of them. Piaget turned to it as a model of the adolescent's hypothetico-deductive thinking, of which the hallmark is the ability to take into account all possible combinations of events.

To give a very simple example of the workings of the lattice structure, let us suppose that a school administrator, faced with the problems of integration, wanted to consider every possible arrangement for grouping white and black boys and girls in the first grade. Operating on the concrete level, he might simply tally up the number of white girls, of black girls, of white boys, and of black boys (four propositions). Then he might assign them to first-grade classes in equal numbers. But if he were operating at the hypothetico-deductive level of thought, he might want to consider all the possible arrangements for any particular classroom. These would include the following:

1. No children at all
2. White boys only
3. White girls only
4. Black boys only
5. Black girls only
6. White boys and white girls
7. Black boys and black girls
8. White boys and black girls
9. Black boys and white girls
10. Girls only, white and black
11. Boys only, white and black

12. White boys and girls, and black boys
13. White boys and girls, and black girls
14. Black boys and girls, and white boys
15. Black boys and girls, and white girls
16. White boys and girls, and black boys and girls

This lattice of sixteen possible combinations, while it may not represent practical solutions, at least gives the harried administrator the satisfaction of knowing that he has considered all the logical possibilities open to him. If none of them seems desirable, he may want to go back and reconsider the first proposition. Or he may find it simpler to resign! In any case, by following the formal reasoning of this logical structure and ignoring the impractical content, our administrator has shown himself capable of operating at the level of pure thought, regardless of the demands of civil rights groups and his PTA.

Using the lattice as a model, Inhelder and Piaget devised an experiment that showed the adolescent's ability to deal with all possible combinations in a systematic fashion. They set up four similar flasks containing colorless, odorless liquids which looked alike but were quite different in chemical composition. One contained water, another dilute sulfuric acid, a third oxygenated water, and the last thiosulfate. There was also a bottle of potassium iodide equipped with a medicine dropper (top row, Figure 10). Since oxygenated water oxidizes potassium iodide in an acid medium, a mixture of oxygenated water, sulfuric acid, and potassium iodide will produce a yellow fluid. Inhelder and Piaget presented their subjects with two glasses, one containing water and the other a mixture of sulfuric acid and oxygenated water. To each glass they added a few drops of potassium iodide (bottom row, Figure 10). The liquid in one glass, of course, turned yellow; in the other it remained clear. Had the thiosulfate been added to the first glass it would

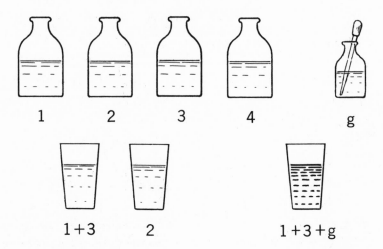

Figure 10 The four similar flasks in the top row contain colorless, chemically different liquids: (1) dilute sulphuric acid, (2) water, (3) oxygenated water, (4) thiosulphate. The small flask (g) contains potassium oxide. The two glasses below are presented to the child; one contains 1 + 3, the other 2. The liquid in the first glass turns yellow when the experimenter adds several drops of g; the liquid in the second glass remains colorless when several drops of g are added to it.

From Inhelder and Piaget, *Growth of Logical Thinking*, p. 108.

have bleached out the color. The youngsters were then asked to make the yellow "syrup" by combining the substances in any way they chose.

The preoperational children combined two elements at a time without any systematic procedure or any proof of the results. Their hypotheses were guesswork: "Maybe it's because the water changes," or "Maybe the color melted." The children at the concrete level began by combining potassium iodide (g) with liquid from each of the four flasks, but it did not occur to them to go beyond pairs of combinations until the experimenter suggested it.

Ren (7;1) tries $4 \times g$, then $2 \times g$, $1 \times g$, and $3 \times g$: *"I think I did everything. . . . I tried them all.* What else could you have done? *I don't know."* We give him the glasses again: he repeats $1 \times g$, etc. "You took each bottle separately. What else could you have done? *Take two bottles at the same time*" (he tries 1 × 4 × g, then 2 × 3 × g, thus failing to cross over between the two sets [of bottles], for example 1 × 2, 1 × 3, 2 × 4, and 3 × 4). When we suggest that he add others, he puts 1 × g in the glass already containing 2 × 3 which results in the appearance of the color: "Try to make the color again. *Do I put in two or three?* (he tries with 2 × 4 × g, then adds 3, then tries it with 1 × 4 × 2 × g). *No, I don't remember any more,*" etc.[5]

Here it is interesting to see that Ren came upon the correct combination only through luck and experimental prodding. Once he hit upon it, he couldn't remember how he achieved it!

Gradually, however, the older children began to construct two-by-two or three-by-three combinations. Sometimes, after adding g to the contents of each flask separately, a youngster would put the combinations together and thus get the yellow color fortuitously or discover how to bleach it out.

Kis (9;6) begins with (3 × g) + (1 × g) + (2 × g) + (4 × g), after which he spontaneously mixes the contents of the four glasses in another glass; but there are no further results. "*O.K., we start over again.*" This time he mixes 4 × g first, then 1 × g: "*No result.*" Then he adds 2 × g, looks and finally puts in 3 × g. "*Another try* (1 × g, then 2 × g, then 3 × g). *Ah!* (yellow appeared, but he adds 4 × g). *Oh! so that! So that's* [4] *what takes away the color. 3 gives the best color.* Can you make the color with fewer bottles? *No.* Try" (he undertakes several 2-by-2 combinations, but at random).[6]

Finally, around twelve or thirteen, the youngsters began to work in a systematic way, taking into consideration all possible *n*-by-*n* combinations.

Cha (13;0) : "*You have to try with all the bottles. I'll begin with the one at the end* (from 1 to 4 with g). *It doesn't work any more. Maybe you have to mix them* (he tries 1 × 2 × g, then 1 × 3 × g). *It turned yellow. But are there other solutions? I'll try* (1 × 4 × g; 2 × 3 × g; 2 × 4 × g; 3 × 4 × g; with the

two preceding combinations this gives the six two-by-two combinations systematically). *It doesn't work. It only works with* (1 × 3 ×
g). Yes, and what about 2 and 4? *2 and 4 don't make any color
together. They are negative. Perhaps you could add 4 in 1 × 3 × g
to see if it would cancel out the color* (he does this). *Liquid 4
cancels it all. You'd have to see if 2 has the same influence* (he
tries it). *No, so 2 and 4 are not alike, for 4 acts on 1 × 3 and 2
does not.* What is there in 2 and 4? *In 4 certainly water. No, the
opposite, in 2 certainly water since it doesn't act on the liquids;
that makes things clearer.* And if I were to tell you that 4 is water?
*If this liquid 4 is water, when you put it with 1 × 3 it wouldn't
completely prevent the yellow from forming. It isn't water; it's
something harmful.*"[7]

Here we see a complete difference in attitude, shown in the
logical approach to the problem and the understanding that
the color results from the combinations of elements. The final
phase occurs when a youngster establishes that the color is due
to a combination of 1 × 3 × g, and then experiments with 2
and 4 to verify which one will bleach out the color. Here, "the
combinatorial system becomes an instrument of conclusive
deduction."[8]

The development of logical thinking demonstrated in this
experiment is a good example of what Piaget means when he
says that organization is inherent in intellectual functioning
and imposes its structure on thought. He then raises the question of what brings about these progressive restructurings of
thought which we have observed at the various developmental
levels. The children's responses, at least at the formal level, bear
such similarity to the approaches to problem solving taught in
school that it might be thought that adolescent structures of
thought were imposed by education.

Piaget rejects this argument flatly. "Society does not act on
growing individuals simply by external pressure, and the individual is not, in relation to the social any more than to the

physical environment, a simple *tabula rasa* on which social constraint imprints ready-made knowledge. For, if the social milieu is really to influence individual brains, they have to be in a state of readiness to assimilate its contributions."[9]

Here Piaget reiterates his position that formal structures are neither innate and "inscribed in advance" on the nervous system nor created by a society which imposes them on the individual from outside. Rather, they are forms of equilibrium which arise out of the interchange between adolescents and other people, and between them and the physical world in which they develop. Mature cerebral structures are a necessary part of this interchange—necessary, but not sufficient. For "between the nervous system and society there is individual activity—i.e., the sum of the experience of an individual in learning to adapt to both physical and social worlds."[10]

We have seen this "individual activity" develop from the simple coordinations of reflexes at the sensory-motor level to the logical, systematic consideration of all hypothetical possibilities at the level of formal thought. Probably the most fascinating thing about reading Piaget is that he makes us aware of the rhythm inherent in the process of growth, beginning with the repetition of the primary circular reactions and continuing through the entire cycle of development. The physical tasks which the child faces at the sensory-motor level (e.g., learning to walk) are repeated at the symbolic level of the preoperational child (e.g., learning to talk). The young child can deal with concrete objects; the schoolchild can deal with them in thought; the adolescent is freed from the bonds of physical reality to soar into the realm of hypothetical possibilities. The process of equilibration is repeated at each level of development. There is a period of puzzling, of searching for new and better adjustments, of striving to achieve a balance between past experience and present uncertainties. When equilibrium is established in one area, the restless organism begins to explore in another. This is the common characteristic of all living beings, as Piaget sees them. At every biological and intellectual level there is an urge toward adaptation, understanding, and mastery. Far from being "empty organisms" reacting passively to stimulus and shock, human beings are active explorers, adjusting to the world as they find it, but also modifying the world to meet their needs.

It becomes clear as we look back that for all his emphasis on discrete stages, Piaget views development as continuous and consistent. Each stage evolves out of the one before it and contributes to the following one. Some children mature faster than others, but the sequence is unchanging. Moreover, development is horizontal as well as vertical. The structures of thought at each level are richer, more complex, more inclusive. Piaget's life has been a never-ending search for these underlying "structures d'ensemble," or structures of the whole, which exemplify the organizing and integrating properties of cognitive development.

Development is continuous for Piaget not only within the individual but throughout all evolutionary levels. From the biological to the social to the intellectual level, the unity of nature is preserved in his theory. The functioning of the lowliest mollusk is based on the same fundamental processes as that of an Einstein. We will see these processes of assimilation and accommodation repeated over and over again as we turn now to the consideration of the child's adaptive development in a number of specific areas.

9

morality

The essence of morality is respect for a system of rules. Most of these rules are handed down from parent to child, but in the case of children's games, the rules are passed from older children to younger ones. So, to study the development of morality at this simplest social level, Piaget got down on his knees and played marbles with little Swiss boys. He found that even in this elementary game different rules, rituals, and expressions were used in different parts of Switzerland and that most children were aware of these variations. How they adapted themselves to these rules and how they looked upon them were the questions to which Piaget sought answers in an effort to cast light on the development of moral attitudes in children.

In the very earliest stages of play with marbles, Piaget observed only motor manipulation, with no consciousness of rules. He described his three-year-old daughter, Jacqueline, digging a "little nest" in the ground in which she buried the "baby balls." Preschool children of four or five would imitate the rules for playing marbles by drawing a square in the ground but would play in an egocentric way, either by themselves or with others. Their understanding of the rules consisted only of going through the accepted motions, with individual variations as fancy dictated. These were the children who would say, "We've both won!"

Around the ages of seven or eight, however, Piaget noted that the children became increasingly aware of the rules of the game. These were regarded as sacred and unchangeable, invented by daddies, God, or "the gentlemen of the Town Council." Piaget investigated the children's attitudes toward rules by asking questions. How did rules begin? Can they be changed? Have rules always been the same as they are today? Here are the answers of one small boy, Fal, to Piaget's questions.

Fal (5) . . . "Long ago when people were beginning to build the town of Neuchâtel, did little children play at marbles the way you showed me?—*Yes.*—Always that way?—*Yes.*—How did you get to know the rules?—*When I was quite little my brother showed me. My Daddy showed my brother.*—And how did your daddy know?—*My Daddy just knew. No one told him.*—How did he know?—*No one showed him!*—Am I older than your Daddy?— *No, you're young. My Daddy had been born when we came to Neuchâtel. My Daddy was born before me.*—Tell me some people older than your daddy.—*My grand-dad.*—Did he play marbles?— *Yes.*—Then he played before your daddy?—*Yes, but not with rules!* [said with great conviction].—What do you mean by rules?— . . . [Fal does not know this word, which he has just heard from our lips for the first time. But he realizes that it means an essential property of the game of marbles; that is why he asserts so emphatically that his grand-dad did not play with rules so as to show how superior his daddy is to everyone else in the world.]—

Was it a long time ago when people played for the first time?—
Oh, yes.—How did they find out how to play?—*Well, they took
some marbles, and then they made a square, and then they put the
marbles inside it* . . . etc. [he enumerates the rules that he
knows].—Was it little children who found out or grown-up gentlemen?—*Grown-up gentlemen.*—Tell me who was born first, your
daddy or your grand-dad?—*My Daddy was born before my grand-
dad.*—Who invented the game of marbles?—*My Daddy did.*—Who
is the oldest person in Neuchâtel?—*I dunno.*—Who do you think?
—*God.*—Did people know how to play marbles before your
daddy?—*Other gentlemen played* [before? at the same time?].
—In the same way as your daddy?—*Yes.*—How did they know
how to?—*They made it up.*—Where is God?—*In the sky.*—Is he
older than your daddy? *Not so old.*—Could one find a new way
of playing?—*I can't play any other way.*—Try . . . [Fal does not
move]. Couldn't you put them like this [we place the marbles in a
circle without a square]?—*Oh, yes.*—Would it be fair?—*Oh, yes.*
—As fair as the square?—*Yes.*—Did your daddy use to play that
way or not?—*Oh, yes.*—Could one play still other ways?—*Oh,
yes.*" We then arrange the marbles in the shape of a T, we put them
in a matchbox, etc. Fal says he has never seen this done before,
but that it is all quite fair and that you can change things as much
as you like. Only his daddy knows all this![1]

This little boy expressed great respect for rules, which he
attributed to his father, who was older and wiser than either
God or his grandfather. Rules to him were endowed with divine
right; when he was shown a new way of playing, he felt that he
was merely rediscovering what his father already knew. This
represents the attitude which Piaget calls *the morality of constraint*. Rules are first made for children by adults; and children, when they are small and dependent, accept them as final
and inviolable. Many of the children questioned by Piaget expressed more resistance than Fal to any change in the rules.

After about ten years of age, however, Piaget noted a complete transformation in children's attitudes toward rules. They
became no longer sacred laws laid down by adults, but decisions

made by the children who played the games. They depended upon local custom and agreement among the players and could be changed at will, so long as everyone agreed. This attitude toward rules Piaget calls *the morality of cooperation;* it is illustrated by this interview:

Ross (11) belongs to the third stage in regard to the practice of rules. He claims that he often invents new rules with his playmates: *"We make them* [up] *sometimes. We go up to 200. We play about and then hit each other, and then he says to me: 'If you go up to 100 I'll give you a marble.'* Is this new rule fair like the old ones, or not?—*Perhaps it isn't quite fair, because it isn't very hard to take four marbles that way!*—If everyone does it, will it be a real rule, or not?—*If they do it often, it will become a real rule.*—Did your father play the way you showed me, or differently?—*Oh, I don't know. It may have been a different game. It changes. It still changes quite often.*—Have people been playing for long?—*At least fifty years.*—Did people play marbles in the days of the 'Old Swiss'?—*Oh, I don't think so.*—How did it begin?—*Some boys took some motor balls* (ball bearings) *and then they played. And after that there were marbles in shops.*—Why are there rules in the game of marbles?—*So as not to be always quarrelling you must have rules, and then play properly*—How did these rules begin?—*Some boys came to an agreement amongst themselves and made them.*—Could you invent a new rule?—*Perhaps* . . . [he thinks] *you put three marbles together and you drop another from above on to the middle one.*—Could one play that way?—*Oh, yes.*—Is that a fair rule like the others?—*The chaps might say it wasn't very fair because it's luck. To be a good rule, it has to be skill.*—But if everyone played that way, would it be a fair rule or not?—*Oh, yes, you could play just as well with that rule as with the others."*[2]

In this example we see a great change in attitude; respect for rules is now based upon mutual consent and cooperation, whereas in the younger boy, Fal, rules were based on unilateral respect and the acceptance of commands received from powerful elders.

From a consideration of these two positions exemplified in

children's games, Piaget went on to study the development of moral judgment in children. He did this by presenting pairs of stories illustrating different degrees of responsibility for damage done. For example, in one story a child accidentally knocks over a tray and breaks fifteen cups. In its companion story, a boy climbing up to steal jam out of a cupboard, against his mother's orders, knocks over one cup which falls on the floor and breaks.

In comparing responses to these pairs of stories, Piaget found that children under the age of ten tended to measure the gravity of the deed in terms of the amount of damage done. Thus the child who broke fifteen cups deserved a greater punishment than the one who broke only one, because by objective standards his was the greater guilt. This view Piaget considers a direct outgrowth of what he calls *moral realism,* which "demands that the letter rather than the spirit of the law shall be observed."[3] Moral realism, he feels, grows out of adult constraint; rules are given to children ready-made and external to subjective feelings. China is expensive and it is forbidden to break cups; regardless of the child's motives, the one who breaks fifteen cups is objectively responsible for much more damage than the child who breaks only one. In this view the child is reflecting the values which have been communicated to him by adults who become angry and scold him for breaking, soiling, or spoiling objects. This attitude is inculcated very early in children and is stronger in some than in others, depending upon how angry the parents become at their children's unintended clumsiness or "accidents" during toilet training. Some children feel they must clean up their plates, hungry or not; or become very concerned about dirtying their clothes. Piaget shows how even mild and loving parents who do not lay down categorical rules somehow communicate this sense of "objective responsibility" to their youngsters. He describes how upset

Jacqueline was at the age of two when she was given a diar-
rhetic, even though she had been warned about its effects: "Her
face assumes an expression of distress, her eyes fill with tears,
her mouth droops, and she is obviously experiencing the same
feelings as if the thing had happened in normal circumstances
through her own negligence."[4]

At about ten years of age, however, children gradually lose
this sense of objective responsibility and begin to place more
emphasis on subjective intentions. Then the child who did not
mean to break the cups is excused, while the one who was deliberately disobeying or who intentionally spilled ink or stole
candy in a store becomes the more guilty one. Piaget argues
that the answers children gave to his stories express "two distinct moral attitudes—one that judges actions according to
their material consequences, and one that takes only intentions
into account. These two attitudes may co-exist at the same age
and even in the same child, but broadly speaking, they do not
synchronize. Objective responsibility diminishes on the average as the child grows older, and subjective responsibility gains
correlatively in importance."[5]

The same developmental process can be seen in children's
attitudes toward lying and stealing. The youngest children
Piaget questioned did not even know what a lie was. It was
"words you mustn't say"; "naughty words"; "when you talk
nonsense." In other words, a lie is something parents don't
approve of. Piaget found that by about seven children knew
that a lie was an untruth. However, they still did not always
discriminate between a deliberate lie and an error. The following is Piaget's account of interviews with two youngsters:

Mab (6): "What is a lie?—*When you talk nonsense.*—You tell
me about something that is a lie.—*A boy once said he was a little
angel, and it wasn't true.*—Why did he say that?—*For a joke.*—
Are we allowed to tell lies?—*No.*—Why not?—*Because it's a sin*

and God doesn't want us to sin.—A boy told me that $2 + 2 = 5$. Is it true?—*No, it makes 4.*—Was it a lie or did he make a mistake? —*He made a mistake.*—Is making a mistake the same as telling a lie or different?—*The same.*—Look at me. I'm 30. A boy told me I was 60. Was it a lie or did he make a mistake?—*It was a lie.*— Why?—*Because what he said was a sin.*—Which is naughtiest, to make a mistake or to tell a lie?—*Both the same.*"

Chap (7) : "What is a lie?—*What isn't true, what they say that they haven't done.*—Guess how old I am.—*Twenty.*—No, I'm thirty. Was it a lie what you told me?—*I didn't do it on purpose.* —I know. But is it a lie all the same, or not?—*Yes, it is all the same, because I didn't say how old you really were.*—Is it a lie?— *Yes, because I didn't speak the truth.*—Ought you to be punished? —*No.*—Was it naughty or not naughty?—*Not so very naughty.*— Why?—*Because I spoke the truth afterwards!*"[6]

Many of the younger children evaluated lies objectively; the bigger the story, the worse the sin. The same held true of stealing: a boy who stole a roll was worse than a girl who stole a ribbon in the companion story, because "rolls cost more"; or "the roll is bigger than the ribbon." A very clear indication of how objective responsibility arises out of constraints exercised by adults is seen in the children's feeling that you mustn't tell lies "because you get punished." Piaget told one story in which two children each broke a cup and lied about their responsibility. One mother believed her child and didn't punish him; the other mother did. "Are both lies that they told equally naughty?" asked Piaget. "No," said some children. "Which is the naughtiest?" "The one who was punished," came the answer. Piaget also reported that a little girl at the Maison des Petits told a lie and was asked by her teacher if that was right. "It doesn't matter," said the child. "My mummy can't see."

Gradually, however, children's attitudes toward lies show progress in the direction of mutual trust and respect. From being wrong because it is "naughty" and the object of punishment, a lie becomes something wrong in itself; the bigger the lie, the worse the wrong. Finally, a lie is seen as wrong because it is in conflict with mutual trust and understanding. The children realize that what is bad about a lie is that "you can't believe in it." As one ten-year-old expressed it, "You can't trust people any more."

According to Piaget, the early stage of moral realism is a "natural and spontaneous product of child thought." It is closely related to the realism in nature which we discussed in Chapter 6. If clouds move because they "must hurry" and the sun shines in the day because it is "not allowed" out at night, it is only a short step to the moral realism we have described; children must clean up their plates and brush their teeth and not disobey their parents. The morality is in the external rules, just as the lie is in being caught. Thus the parents are the source of moral realism; and the stricter the parents, the greater the objective responsibility the child feels. And as Piaget says, "The majority of parents are poor psychologists and give their children the most questionable of moral trainings. It is perhaps in this domain that one realizes most keenly how immoral it can be to believe too much in morality, and how much more precious is a little humanity than all the rules in the world."[7]

How then do children develop from a morality based on parental constraint to one based on mutual cooperation? To cast light upon this question, Piaget takes up the development of the idea of justice in punishment. For he notes that "it is often at the expense of the adult and not because of him that the notions of just and unjust find their way into the youthful mind."[8] Children, particularly after they enter school, develop a strong sense of solidarity with their peer group. They stand united against what they consider "unfair," and those who are "tattletales" soon find themselves excommunicated from the group. And this is precisely the age at which "the equalitarian notion of justice begins to assert itself with sufficient strength to overcome the authority of the adult."[9]

Piaget began his study of justice in his usual disarming way. "You know," he said, "it isn't at all easy to know how to punish children so as to be quite fair. Lots of fathers and teachers don't know how to. So I thought I would ask the children themselves, you and your friends. I shall tell you all sorts of silly things that little children have done, and you'll tell me how you think they ought to be punished."[10] Then he told a story of some childish misbehavior, followed by three possible punishments. He asked his listeners how they would have punished the young offender, and analyzed the results.

The earliest concept of justice, Piaget found, was based on retribution. The child who has misbehaved must be punished, and to the younger children the fairest punishment is the most severe. It may be an arbitrary kind of punishment, which bears no relation to the misdeed (being spanked or deprived of some outing) but makes expiation for it. Or the punishment may grow out of the consequences of the misdeed, such as being put to bed when one has pretended to be ill; this Piaget called *punishment by reciprocity*. The older children favored the latter, which would include the ancient Talon Law, "An eye for an eye and a tooth for a tooth." The younger ones, at least in discussing *other* children, favored the most strict or painful expiatory punishment. As one child said, "He ought to be stopped doing what he liked doing best."[11]

Piaget felt that these two attitudes toward punishment corresponded to the two levels of morality. Adult constraints produce expiatory punishment based on the objective degree of damage; but punishment based on equality and mutual cooperation is reciprocal and takes motives and subjective responsibility into consideration. There even comes a time in this latter stage when children feel that punishment is not necessary, that explanation is sufficient "because I can understand much better when people explain things to me," as one boy put it.

In studying children's attitudes toward justice, Piaget came across an interesting phenomenon. He found among young children the notion that justice is immanent in the natural order of things; that knives cut children who have been forbidden to use them or that old bridges give way under children who cross them to steal apples. This would seem to be a residue of the magic omnipotence of early childhood (see Chapter 6). As Piaget puts it,

. . . it seems quite natural to the child that a fault should automatically bring about its own punishment. For nature, in the child's eyes, is not a system of blind forces regulated by mechanical laws operating on the principle of chance. Nature is a harmonious whole, obeying laws that are as much moral as physical and that are above all penetrated down to the least detail with an anthropomorphic or even egocentric finalism. It therefore seems quite natural to little children that night should come in order to put us to sleep, and that the act of going to bed is sufficient to set in motion that great black cloud that produces darkness. It seems quite natural to them that their movements should command those of the heavenly bodies (the moon follows us in order to take care of us). In short, there is life and purpose in everything. Why then should not things be the accomplices of grownups in making sure that a punishment is inflicted where the parents' vigilance may have been evaded?[12]

From the age of about eight on, this early belief in immanent justice tends to disappear slowly, though occasionally we find traces of it among uneducated people, or those religious individuals who say, "God is punishing you." Children who masturbate often have fantasies that their health or their intelligence may be affected as a result of their forbidden habits.

Piaget cites the case of his psychiatrist friend who had a vivid childhood memory of the cover of a basket unexpectedly closing on his hand when he was reaching inside for apples. He was doing no wrong, but he was immediately overcome with a sense of guilt and felt that he was being caught and punished. Piaget feels that "belief in immanent justice originates . . . in a transference to things of feelings acquired under the influence of adult constraint."[13] As the child grows older and sees that "wickedness may go unpunished and virtue remain unrewarded," his belief in immanent justice gradually fades away.

We have already discussed the second stage of "retributive justice," during which children believe punishment is the necessary retribution for disobeying their elders. As they grow older and form groups in school they learn to put equality of treatment and mutual cooperation above punishment and to be more aware of individual motives and circumstances. These are the youngsters who make allowances for the clumsiness of little children or for those who are doing something wrong for the sake of someone else. Piaget feels that most children by eleven or twelve years of age have progressed to this third or final phase of "distributive justice." This consists of taking account of varying degrees of responsibility—not only inner motives but factors such as age and experience. Youngsters who have reached this stage will give little children who are just learning a game an extra try or overlook accidental errors.

Piaget closes his study of morality with an interesting sociological analysis of how morality based on cooperation can develop out of a childhood morality based on parental authoritarianism. As we have already seen, children are basically egocentric; their understanding of right and wrong is based on their own distorted perceptions and a reification of their parents' commands. But in the course of all the spontaneous

give and take that occurs within families and among playmates, children gradually move outside their egocentrism and
come to see another person's point of view. They begin to
think of right and wrong in terms of the circumstances of the
person involved rather than in terms of "retributive justice."
Just as the mountain looked different to Laurent when he saw
it from another perspective, so moral sanctions appear different
in differing circumstances. Adult authority is not sufficient to
create in children a true sense of justice. As Piaget points out,
this is a situation which is not in equilibrium and therefore
cannot be stable. The adult is strong and demanding; the child
feels weak and inferior. Unilateral respect leads only to moral
constraint. The factor essential to moral development is mutual
respect and cooperation—"cooperation between children to
begin with, and then between child and adult as the child approaches adolescence, and comes, secretly at least, to consider
himself as the adult's equal."[14]

Piaget thus leads us to see that it is the growth of strong
moral solidarity among grade-school children that brings about
equilibrium, an equilibrium based on mutual respect and consideration. Wise parents and teachers have always been aware
of this and, by being gentle, considerate, and fair with children,
have achieved much happier results than those who have ruled
by authority. In these troubled days, when the youth of our
land are revolting against all forms of moral constraint and
discipline from above, there may be lessons for us in Piaget's
gentle philosophy. If the young people can be brought to see
that the need for "law and order" is as much theirs as their
elders', if the generations can work together in mutual respect
and cooperation, we may once again have greater harmony in
our land.

10

emotional development

Piaget says comparatively little about the child's emotional life, and he scatters his observations in paragraphs or short chapters here and there in his books. In comparison with most modern theories of personality, his ideas are limited and inadequate. He obviously has given much less thought to this aspect of personality than he has to cognitive or even perceptual functioning. However, his statements are worth thinking about, and so we present them for consideration.

Piaget does not overlook or deny the importance of feelings —*affects* is the term he uses—but he has focused his interest primarily on the growth of intelligence, which he views as central in the life of each person. He concedes, however, that every intelligent act is accompanied by feelings (of interest, pleasure, effort, etc.) and that these feelings provide the energy that sparks intellectual growth. Emotion is what makes intelligence dynamic, directed, ever seeking a better equilibrium; emotion and intelligence are two sides of the same coin. "What common sense calls 'feelings' and 'intelligence,' regarding them as two opposed 'faculties,' are simply behavior relating to persons and behavior affecting ideas or things; but in each of these forms of behavior, the same affective and cognitive aspects of action emerge, aspects which are in fact always associated and in no way represent independent faculties."[1]

For Piaget, then, every action involves a structural or cognitive aspect and an energetic or affective aspect. Intelligence provides the structure for actions while feelings provide the dynamics. Since the two are interdependent, emotional development requires the same continuing process of adaptation as cognitive development. Emotions have to assimilate new situations from the outer world and accommodate to them to create new "affective schemata," or ways of responding. If a baby finds a person who loves him, he grows affectionate toward that person; if he meets rejection or hostility, he develops aggressive tendencies. But even these emotional responses involve intelligence and reasoning. "Personal schemas, like all others, are both intellectual and affective. We do not love without seeking to understand, and we do not even hate without a subtle use of judgment. Thus when we speak of 'affective schemas' it must be understood that what is meant is merely the affective aspect of schemas which are also intellectual."[2]

In a recently translated paper, Piaget traces the parallel between emotional and intellectual life throughout childhood and adolescence.[3] He consistently refers to the motivational aspects of behavior (interest, curiosity, will, determination) and the value systems (moral standards, ideals, goals, aspirations) as part of emotional life. So in describing the emotional life of the infant, Piaget includes not only the primary emotional reflexes of love, rage, and fear but also the instinctive strivings of the infant for food and comfort. He shows how the growing baby strives to achieve pleasure and avoid pain through his sensory-motor actions, thereby gratifying his own body and his primitive ego, which is not even aware of other people at this point. The whole development of object constancy, which we have previously discussed, is here very closely related to Freud's concept of "object-choice." As the baby realizes that his mother exists as a separate person and that she is the source of food, warmth, dry diapers, and all his primitive gratifications, he comes to love her more and himself less. He turns from narcissistic self-interest to increased awareness of his mother, and then of others in his external world. His mother becomes his first love-object—or "object-choice," to use psychoanalytic terminology. Through her he learns to differentiate between himself and external reality; not only intellectually as we have already discussed, but emotionally as well. He becomes interested in pleasing her (the dawn of motivation) and aware of her moods, which he reflects. This is the beginning of the child's emotional as well as his intellectual life.

At this point we must discuss Piaget's use of the word "ego." He speaks of the ego as the primitive sense of self, not as selfish but simply unaware of others. Egocentrism is not the same as egotism, as we have pointed out before. But in describing the primitive ego of babies, which at one point Piaget even calls "detestable,"[4] he seems to be referring to what Freud calls the "id"—the lowest level of consciousness, concerned with primary gratification and primitive emotions.

At the preoperational level, Piaget describes an emerging sense of self-in-relation-to-others, which more nearly fits the Freudian definition of "ego." The child at this period, he says, acquires new interests and values, shows emerging moral sentiments, and develops interpersonal emotions beyond the range of his immediate family. His newly developing interests are an outgrowth of the primitive needs of babyhood, extended now to include interest in drawing pictures, in learning new words, and in all the symbolic activities that are part of his intellectual growth at this stage.

The amount of interest and motivation that the child shows is closely connected with his self-image. If the image of himself which he sees reflected back to him in his mother's eyes, in his family's attitudes, in the way he is treated by other children, is warm and positive, he will see himself as a "good" person. The way he behaves, the confidence with which he tackles new problems, the interest he shows in learning new things—all are a function of his self-image. His attitude about himself is reflected in his emotional responses to other people. He may be a happy, loving, outgoing youngster, quick to sympathize with others, willing to share his toys and get along with his playmates. Or he may be anxious, sullen, withdrawn, or hostile, thereby expressing his anger and fear at the way the world has treated him. The foundations for future learning are laid in these tremendously important preschool years, and though Piaget does not say so, both cognitive and emotional development may be permanently damaged during this period.

We have seen in our discussion of the morality of the young child that respect for adults is the source of the earliest moral feelings. Respect, says Piaget, "consists of affection and fear, and fear is the reason for the inequality in such an affective relationship."[5] Thus lies to adults are prohibited, but not lies to one's playmates. This is the morality of constraint, which we have discussed; rules are made by adults and justice is based on the Talon Law (an eye for an eye; a tooth for a tooth). Adults, at this period of a child's life, are extremely important to his emotional and moral development.

This importance slowly declines, however, as youngsters

enter the middle years of childhood. When they become intellectually capable of seeing another person's point of view, they also become emotionally empathetic. "Cooperation among individuals coordinates their points of view into a reciprocity which assures both the autonomy of the individual and the cohesion of the group."[6] Mutual respect among youngsters changes their moral feelings: rules depend on cooperation, and justice becomes "distributive." One who lies to his peers or tattles on them now becomes a social outcast. The morality of cooperation, a higher form of equilibrium, has at this stage replaced the morality of submission to authority.

The other hallmark of this stage of emotional development, says Piaget, is the appearance of will power. Will is the final outgrowth of childish needs and interests. Piaget compares its function to that of logical operations; it represents a stable equilibrium of organized emotions. When there is a conflict of emotions (the desire for pleasure, for example, as opposed to the demands of duty), will power reinforces "the superior but weaker tendency so as to make it triumph."[7] As such, it is a regulator of energy, reinforcing the superior choice just as logical reasoning reinforces the correct deduction which is in conflict with perceptual appearance. Thus, will power helps one stay on a diet when tempted by chocolate cake, just as logic helps one to know that a ball of clay remains the same, no matter how much larger it looks when flattened out.

In adolescence, Piaget finds the major emotional achievements are the development of personality and of ideals. He more or less dismisses the emotional changes brought on by puberty and says that the fundamental problem of adolescence is that the individual begins to take up adult roles. This means he has to discipline himself to goals and ideals. For Piaget, "personality is the submission of the ego to an ideal which it embodies but which goes beyond it and subordinates it."[8] A strong personality is one which is able to discipline the ego by opposing it. Whereas the ego is self-centered, personality is "the decentered ego."

What Piaget is saying here is that the child has a limited ability to understand and cooperate with others. He relates to his own peers and comprehends concrete experiences such as personal injustices he may have suffered. But he is unable to relate to humanity as a whole or to comprehend abstract ideals such as patriotism or social justice. That is why personality, according to Piaget's definition, does not emerge until adolescence, although it has its roots in the development of will during middle childhood. The child is not capable of constructing theories and analyzing his own thinking. Nor is he much concerned about people outside of his own familiar circle. But the adolescent can think beyond the present and the familiar, to build political ideologies or philosophical systems. He is a dreamer of dreams, a righter of wrongs, a defender of civil liberties and political freedom. He tends to have nothing but contempt for the society which produced him, and sometimes his plans are tinged with megalomania. He may attribute to himself an essential role in the salvation of humanity, or take part in radical movements, like so many of the students of today's generation.

The cure for the adolescent's untempered idealism, says Piaget, is work—"effective enduring work, undertaken in concrete and well-defined situations, cure[s] all dreams."[9] Just as experience reconciles hypothetical possibilities with the practical reality of things, so professional work restores equilibrium and "marks the advent of adulthood."

Could it be that Piaget is telling us how to deal with the young revolutionaries of today? The alienated college students, who are dropping out and searching for identity, might find it much faster if they had jobs, adult responsibilities, and families to support. There would be fewer dropouts in our society if parents did not send them monthly allowances. Perhaps the answer is that in our culture adult roles are postponed too long. Young people have the privileges of adulthood without the responsibilities. Piaget's words were written in 1940, but his message is relevant today. "One should not be disquieted by the extravagance and disequilibrium of the better part of adolescence. . . . True adaptation to society comes automatically when the adolescent reformer attempts to put his ideas to work."[10]

11

play and imitation

Play, according to Piaget, is an indispensable step in the child's cognitive development. Play bridges the gap between sensory-motor experience and the emergence of representative or symbolic thought. Piaget uses the term *ludic symbolism* to describe the "make-believe" games of children in which a stick becomes a gun or a corncob represents a baby doll. The immediate stimulus, the stick or the corncob, is for the child the ludic (playful, jesting) symbol for the gun or doll baby of which he is thinking. Thus the child's make-believe play stimulates the development of his thought about the nonexistent objects which are represented by these symbols. In fact, Piaget suggests that the development of language is also dependent upon the symbolic function of play. First comes the actual sensory-motor experience with an object or action; then comes the make-believe reliving of that experience; and finally comes a word which represents the whole schema verbally. Since language is just beginning at the time when a child's symbolic play is developing, it is difficult to observe definitively which comes first. However, judging by the difficulties of teaching children to read about experiences which they have never had, it would appear that Piaget's hypothesis is correct. Teachers in deprived areas complain about the lack of meaning for ghetto children of the "Dick and Jane" type of readers, and special books have to be written for minority groups. I remember a little boy who could not learn to read the word "night." Far from being deprived in the usual sense, this youngster was over-protected. He was put to bed every night in a room with Venetian blinds and an air conditioner cutting out all the velvety darkness and sleepy sounds of the night. He had never experienced moonlight or starglow; he had no background of meaningful experience, and so he could not learn the verbal symbol "night" which represented all of this.

Play, then, is the child's way of assimilating the reality of the world around him. It bridges the gap between sensory-motor activity and representation in thought. But play—particularly make-believe play—tends to spill over into the realm of fantasy, says Piaget. "Unlike objective thought, which seeks to adapt itself to the requirements of external reality, imaginative play is a symbolic transposition which subjects things to the child's activity, without rules or limitations. It is therefore almost pure assimilation, i.e., thought polarized by preoccupation with individual satisfaction."[1]

If symbolic play is "pure assimilation," Piaget theorizes a balance for it in the process of imitation. Children tend to mimic or imitate anything in their environment. This imitation Piaget defines as "a continuation of accommodation for its own sake."[2] We have already discussed the dual functions of assimilation and accommodation in adaptive functioning. Piaget feels that the baby, by imitating what he sees and hears around him, is accommodating to the reality of his environment. When he plays with that outer reality, happily distorting it to suit his fancy, he is assimilating it to his own past experience. The child who pretends to eat out of an acorn is assimilating the acorn into his experience with dishes and spoons. The child who sits in his high chair imitating the manners and gestures of adults at dinner is accommodating his eating habits to the environment around him.

Of these two processes, imitation seems to come first, although play is often so closely combined with it that it is difficult to say where imitation ceases and play begins. For Piaget the distinction lies in the smiles and signs of pleasure that accompany play, as opposed to the seriousness of the child's attempt to accommodate. Where there is no longer "an effort at comprehension, [but] merely assimilation to the activity itself . . . for the pleasure of the activity, that is play."[3]

Piaget finds evidence of imitative behavior in the very earliest days of a baby's life. He cites the case of his son Laurent, who like many babies began to cry when he heard the wailing of other infants around him in the hospital. The night after he was born, Laurent was awakened by the crying of babies near him and began to cry in chorus with them. This happened several times in the next few days. When Papa Piaget imitated Laurent's whimpering, the baby began to cry in earnest, whereas he made no response when his father whistled or made other kinds of cries.

Piaget attributes this oft-observed phenomenon to a vocal reflex, set off by the crying of the other babies. This would explain why Laurent did not respond to whistle or other noises, but only to crying, which in his state of infantile egocentrism he could not distinguish from his own. While scarcely a conscious imitation, this behavior corresponds to that of the first stage in the development of intelligence, which is characterized by neonatal reflexes, with no awareness of a distinction between self and outer reality.

In the next few months of life Piaget observed *vocal contagion* in all three of his babies, which he has defined as "merely stimulation of the child's voice by another's voice, without exact imitation of the sounds he hears."[4] He describes how he listened to Lucienne's spontaneous sounds at one month old, and how, by systematically imitating them, he was able to get Lucienne to make these sounds in response to his initial sounds. This occurred when she was about three months old.

According to Piaget, vocal contagion develops easily into phonic imitation. The baby responds in some way to the sound of another's voice, then in a vaguely imitative way, and finally, at about six months, in a precise and systematic way. He illustrates this development clearly in the case of Jacqueline, who at six months of age invented a new sound by putting her tongue between her teeth. The sound came out something like *pfs*. Her mother imitated the sound, and Jacqueline, laughing delightedly, repeated it. This went on for three weeks, by which time either father or mother could say *pfs* and Jacqueline would imitate them.

Piaget traces the same developments in the field of vision. He describes how Lucienne, at almost two months, would watch him when he moved his head quickly from left to right, and then reproduce the movement. By two and a half months she could differentiate between sideways and up-and-down movements of his father's head and imitate them accurately. When Piaget went on to more complex motor actions, however, he discovered that a model is imitated only if it can be assimilated to a sensory-motor behavior pattern which has already been formed. For example, Jacqueline, who at six months could reach out and close her fingers around toys, would not imitate her father opening and closing his hand until two months later. Then he observed her alternately opening and closing her fingers, while watching with great attention, as if this were a new and isolated bit of behavior for her. From observations such as this, Piaget concluded that a child can learn to imitate new patterns of motor behavior if they are practiced where he can clearly see them.

This brings up the question of how so many babies can learn to wave "bye-bye" if it is to them a meaningless act which they cannot see themselves perform. Piaget admits that young babies can be trained to do "all kinds of tricks," but he calls this *pseudo-imitation,* not true imitation, requiring constant practice and encouragement by the adult model. Without an enthusiastic example to stimulate such behavior, it is soon forgotten. However, when Daddy waves and smiles every morning when he leaves, or Mommy opens wide her mouth to coax the baby to eat, the child learns early to imitate their behavior and respond to their warm approval.

By eight or nine months of age the baby has reached Stage IV of his sensory-motor development and is ready to learn more complex coordinations of previous behavior patterns. At this time he will imitate movements already familiar but not visible to him, if he has an adult model. He also begins to imitate sounds and gestures that are new to him, with greater flexibility and responsiveness. For example, Lucienne at ten months tried to imitate her father hitting his stomach and lifting a ball. Just under two months later she would imitate him when he hid objects under a handkerchief. Previously she had hidden a rattle under a blanket and had played at looking for hidden objects with her father, but had never hidden the objects herself before.

Piaget explains this interest in new behaviors as a sign of the child's developing intelligence. Up until now he has been interested only in activities which appeared to be a continuation of his own, beginning with the imitation of crying which he could not distinguish from his own, to the attempts to prolong interesting activities by repetitive imitation. Now he is responding in new and more complex ways, stimulated by "models closely enough related to his own activity to provoke the tendency to reproduce, and yet at the same time distinct from his existing schemas."[5]

In the fifth stage of imitation the child, now about one to one and a half years old, begins to imitate new models, varying familiar patterns in different ways, as if to observe different results. This is heard in the child's babbling, where he may go from "da-da" to "ba-ba" to "pa-pa," experimenting with new combinations of sound in an effort to imitate adult phonemes. Or it may appear in motor behavior, such as when Jacqueline imitated her papa drawing lines on a piece of paper. She managed a few strokes with her right hand, and then transferred the pencil to her left. In the process she turned it around, so that when she tried to draw with the wrong end, nothing happened. To encourage her, Piaget went through the motions of making marks with his finger, whereupon Jacqueline promptly imitated him with *her* finger.

The sixth stage of imitation described by Piaget is a very interesting one characterized by *deferred imitation*. Piaget gives several examples in which his children observed something one day, and later imitated it, thus indicating the presence of a mental image of past events.

At 1;4(3) J. had a visit from a little boy of 1;6, whom she used to see from time to time, and who, in the course of the afternoon got into a terrible temper. He screamed as he tried to get out of a play-pen and pushed it backwards, stamping his feet. J. stood

watching him in amazement, never having witnessed such a scene
before. The next day, she herself screamed in her play-pen and
tried to move it, stamping her foot lightly several times in succession. The imitation of the whole scene was most striking. Had it
been immediate, it would naturally not have involved representation, but coming as it did after an interval of more than twelve
hours, it must have involved some representative or pre-representa-
tive element.

At 1;4(17), after a visit from the same boy, she again gave a
clear imitation of him, but in another position. She was standing
up, and drew herself up with her head and shoulders thrown back,
and laughed loudly (like the model).[6]

This incident is reminiscent of Lucienne imitating with her
mouth how to open a matchbox. The children at this stage give
evidence of having mental images or concrete symbols of past
events or invisible objects. They are emerging from the sensory-
motor phase into the long preoperational period in which they
learn to deal with such mental representations.

Overlapping these stages in imitation, and often inseparable
from them, are the beginning stages of play, which Piaget
distinguishes chiefly by *functional pleasure*, expressed in smiles
and laughter, which accompany the activity. In imitation,
as we have said, the child seems to be making a serious effort
to accommodate himself to new objects and activities. In play,
he is assimilating objects and activities to his own satisfaction.
"Just for fun" he builds castles out of sand, or pretends to fly
like Superman. Such activity "is no longer an effort to learn,
it is only a happy display of known actions."[7]

Even Piaget, with all his passion for classification, has difficulty in distinguishing the early stages of play from sensory-
motor behavior in general. He mentions "the pleasure of
feeding time" at the reflex level of the first stage; and at the
second and third stages can only refer to the "ever-increasing
enjoyment" shown by his babies as adaptive behaviors became

easier and more familiar. At the fourth stage he describes how Laurent, who is learning to push aside his father's hand in order to reach a toy, becomes more interested in the contest with his father than in the toy. He pushes aside his father's hand and bursts into laughter, forgetting all about the toy he had been trying to reach! Thus his interest is transferred from the goal of his action to the action itself, and what had been intelligent adaptation has momentarily become play.

During the fifth stage the child characteristically varies familiar behavior patterns in order to observe different results. Piaget says, "It often happens that, by chance, the child combines unrelated gestures without really trying to experiment, and subsequently repeats these gestures as a ritual, and makes a motor game of them."[8] He describes Jacqueline, who at a year old was holding her hair with her right hand during her bath. Her hand, being wet, slipped and struck the water with a splash. This produced an enjoyable new experience which Jacqueline immediately repeated. She varied the height and the position of her hand on her hair, but during succeeding days this behavior pattern was repeated with the regularity of a ritual. Once Jacqueline struck the water as soon as she was put in the bath, but suddenly she stopped and put her hands up to her hair, thus renewing her familiar game.

These behaviors are curious, says Piaget, in that they are not adapted to external circumstances. Such childish rituals are based not on a feeling of compulsion (as older children avoid cracks in the sidewalk, or hit each banister as they pass) but on the pleasure of self-entertainment. Insofar as it goes beyond the necessity for adaptation, such play is seen to be "the function of assimilation."

In the sixth stage, Piaget describes the emergence of *ludic symbolism,* in which an object becomes the symbol for something else which may resemble it only remotely. Jacqueline (aged one year, three months) sees a fringed cloth whose edges remind her of her pillow. She lies down and pretends to go to sleep, laughing all the time. Five months later she pretends to eat a piece of paper, saying, "Very nice." Lucienne, at about the same age, pretended to drink out of a box, and then held it to the mouths of all who were present. This symbolic use of the box had been preceded by playing at drinking out of empty glasses, with all the accompanying noises of lips and throat.

Thus, as early as the beginning of the child's second year, Piaget discerns the "make-believe" games "characteristic of the ludic symbol as opposed to simple motor games."[9] They are also differentiated from imitation in that the function of imitation is to copy or accommodate to the objects of reality, while the function of ludic or symbolic play is to distort the objects of reality to suit the child's fancy. Imitation (based on accommodation to reality) and play (based on assimilating reality to private, egocentric thinking) therefore represent the extremes of the two functions which must work together to achieve equilibrium.

By the end of the sensory-motor period (two years), evidences of imitation and of symbolic play are clearly discernible in Piaget's observations. Both are moving away from dependence on concrete objects in the direction of mental representation, or thought. But in the case of imitation the mental representation is a copy of reality or an image of the object thought of. In the case of ludic play, the object is a symbol which suggests something else existing in the mind of the child. The connection may be obvious or it may be quite remote, depending on how egocentric the child's thinking is. An acorn is an obvious substitute for a dish, but when Jacqueline (at 1;11) slid a shell along a box, only her explanation, "Cat on a wall," made it clear what this symbolized for her. However, the important point is that in either play or imitation the child by the age of two is functioning at the beginning level of thought rather than at the level of sensory-motor activity.

Piaget then goes on to study the evolution of children's play, searching for explanations of it and of why it disappears in later years. He concludes that there are three main categories of play: practice games, symbolic games, and games with rules. Practice games appear first and are an outgrowth of the imitative activities described during the sensory-motor period: pitching pebbles, jumping rope, stringing beads, piling up blocks. Such games may lead simply to improved motor performance or to destructive performance (e.g., knocking over blocks). They may produce new and pleasing results by chance, or by intention, as in the case of many educational games. They may develop into symbolic games, such as building a castle out of sand, or constructive games or even games with rules, such as hopscotch or marbles. Constructive games like building or weaving are regarded by Piaget not really as games, but as a bridge between play and work, merging imperceptibly into the practical skills required in adult life. But games with rules are essentially social, leading to increased adaptation. Piaget feels that since they persist even among adults, they may provide the explanation of what happens to children's play; that it dies out in later years in favor of socialized games.

Most of Piaget's interest, however, centers upon symbolic games, which "imply representation of an absent object" and are both imitative and imaginative. Insofar as these games symbolize for the child his own feelings, interests, and activities, they help him to express himself creatively and to develop a rich and satisfying fantasy life. While Piaget agrees with Freud that children may use make-believe play to express forbidden feelings or unfulfilled wishes, his thinking about the cognitive aspects of such play goes much further. As has been suggested, he feels that ludic symbolism is a necessary step on the way to developing adapted intelligence. When children have completed the long development from sensory-motor activity to operational thought these symbolic games gradually disappear in favor of daydreaming or games with rules.

Between the ages of two (end of the sensory-motor period) and four, symbolic play is at its peak. Piaget, as usual, carefully classified into types and subtypes all the developments he observed in his children's play. Type I includes the projection of the earliest symbolic schemata onto new objects. Jacqueline moved from pretending she was asleep to making her dog and her bear go to sleep. Lucienne pretended to telephone, then made her doll telephone, and finally used all kinds of things, such as a leaf, instead of a real receiver. In the following months the children began to use their bodies to represent other people or things (Type II). Jacqueline at two moved her finger along the table and said, "Finger walking . . . horse trotting." Lucienne was the postman, or her godmother, or "Thérèse with her velvet hat."

At 4;3, L., standing at my side, quite still, imitated the sound of bells. I asked her to stop, but she went on. I then put my hand over her mouth. She pushed me away, angrily, but still keeping very straight and said: *"Don't. I'm a church"* (the belfry).[10]

In the Type I games, says Piaget, the child is trying to "use freely his individual powers, to reproduce his own actions for the pleasure of seeing himself do them, and showing them off to others, in a word to express himself, to assimilate without being hampered by the need to accommodate at the same time."[11] But he soon moves on to Type II games, reproducing other people's looks and actions, or making his toys reproduce his own. In Type III we find the transposition of whole scenes instead of isolated bits, and long, complicated episodes of playacting sometimes sustained over periods of time. At around two and a half Jacqueline pretended to prepare a bath for Lucienne, using an empty box for the bath and a blade of grass as a thermometer. She plunged the thermometer into the bath, and finding it too hot, she waited a moment and tested it again. "That's all right, thank goodness!" she said, and then pretended to undress Lucienne, garment by garment, without actually touching her.

About a month later Jacqueline pretended to be walking a baby to sleep, talking to it as she held it in her arms. A week later, as she played the same game, she stopped talking when anyone came near. From a distance Piaget could hear her saying things like, "Now we're going for a walk." Already Jacqueline's make-believe play was becoming a secret inner experience.

Imaginary companions often appear at this stage of children's symbolic play. Jacqueline at four had a dwarf, followed by a Negress named Marécage. Piaget feels that children create these characters to "provide a sympathetic audience or a mirror for the ego."[12] The characters sometimes acquire some of the moral authority of the parents, thus making it easier for the child to accept parental scoldings in reality. What happens to them? Piaget says that just as children stop talking out loud and "interiorize" their speech (as did Jacqueline in the above observation), so these imaginary characters become interiorized in daydreams.

Piaget also includes *compensatory play* in his discussion of Type III games. This involves doing in make-believe what is forbidden in reality. He describes Jacqueline at 2;4 going through the motions of pouring water with an empty cup after she had been forbidden to play in the real washtub. At 2;7

she wanted to carry Lucienne, who was then a newborn baby. When her mother told her she could not carry the baby yet, Jacqueline folded her arms and announced that she had the baby—there were two babies. Then she rocked and talked to the imaginary baby, and even said she *was* the baby when she was scolded for screaming with temper, thus excusing her behavior. By the time she was four, Jacqueline had a well-developed imagination, and whenever she was restricted in any way, she could make up a "compensatory" tale in which the direction of her desires was clear. When she was angry at her father she announced that Marécage (her imaginary friend) "has a horrid father. He calls her in when she's playing. Her mother chose badly." When she was told to take a nap, Jacqueline said, "Marécage never lies down in the afternoon; she plays all the time." Clearly, she was working out in her make-believe play what was forbidden in reality.

Closely allied to compensatory play is play in which emotion is acted out in gradual degrees, so that it becomes bearable. Freud calls this lessening of emotion through imaginary rehearsal "catharsis"; it has been frequently noted in the play of children who must deal with death or illness or hospitalization, to mention some of the traumas of childhood. Piaget gives the example of Lucienne, who at two was afraid of tractors and planes. "Dolly told me she would like to ride on a machine like that," she said. At three, she remarked that when one of her dolls was a baby, "they gave him a little steam-roller and a tiny tractor."[13] The obvious implication here is that through her dolls Lucienne gained in experience with machines and gradually overcame her fear of them.

Closely related to this is the type of play in which children act out unpleasant scenes or actions. In reliving them by transposing them symbolically, they reduce some of the unpleasantness and make the situations more tolerable. This is the usual explanation of why children enjoy horror movies on TV. They know the scene is not real, that they can turn it off at will, so they are able to cope with the horror and master their own fear in slow degrees. In the following observation Jacqueline shows how a child acts and learns to live with the unpleasant realities of life.

At 3;11(21) J. was impressed by the sight of a dead duck which had been plucked and put on the kitchen table. The next day I found J. lying motionless on the sofa in my study, her arms pressed against her body and her legs bent: "What are you doing, J? Have you a pain? Are you ill? *No, I'm the dead duck.*"

At 4;6, I knocked against J.'s hands with a rake and made her cry. I said how sorry I was, and blamed my clumsiness. At first she didn't believe me, and went on being angry as though I had done it deliberately. Then she suddenly said, half appeased: "*You're Jacqueline and I'm daddy. There!* (she hit my fingers). *Now say: 'You've hurt me.'* (I said it.) *I'm sorry, darling. I didn't do it on purpose. You know how clumsy I am,*" etc. In short, she merely reversed the parts and repeated my exact words.[14]

In these forms of play, as Piaget points out, the child increases his awareness through new experiences or takes his revenge on reality for unpleasant ones. He may even anticipate the results of his actions and construct in his imagination the consequences that would ensue if he disobeyed instructions or got into trouble. Thus, the function of symbolic play is clearly seen in the "make-believe" games of children from two to four. It is "to assimilate reality to the ego, while freeing the ego from the demands of accommodation."[15] This is the age at which the child's fantasy play is the most far-fetched and his view of reality the most distorted. This is probably because he is still bound up in egocentrism and has so many new adjustments to make in such a short time.

During the second half of the preoperational period, symbolic games begin to lose their importance. It is not that they decline so much as that they come closer and closer to reality as the child accommodates to a greater and greater extent to the world around him. Piaget notes that after the age of four, symbolic games become much more orderly, as opposed to the incoherence of earlier games. The child is improving in language skills, and also emerging from the egocentric world of his own needs to the world of reality. He notices how events follow each other in time and space, and his stories become much more precise and coherent.

Another characteristic of play at this age is that it reproduces an increasingly precise imitation of reality. There is "increasing attention to exact detail in the material constructions which accompany these games: houses, cots, tables, kitchens, drawings and models."[16] This is the time when little girls delight in dollhouses complete to the tiniest pots and pans, and boys like realistic forts and guns. Their play becomes increasingly a replica of reality, not only on the level of the setting and properties, but also on the level of what happens in their games. From about five and a half onward, Jacqueline constructed an entire village which she called Ventichon. She, and later Lucienne, spent hours acting out real-life scenes in the lives of its inhabitants—weddings, family visits, dinner parties, and so on. The little girls began to play "permanent parts as mothers of families with numerous children, grandparents, cousins, visitors etc., the husbands being rather in the background. 'Mrs. Odar' and 'Mrs. Anonzo,' etc. thus became the starting point of new cycles, analogous to those of the preceding stages, but much closer to reality, always true to life and with scenery and buildings which became more and more elaborate."[17]

A third characteristic that Piaget notes is that after the age of four or five symbolic play becomes increasingly social. *Collective symbolism* is his term for play in which children take different parts and act them out with an awareness of each other, as in the cases of Mrs. Odar and Mrs. Anonzo above. This is in contrast to the symbolic play of younger children, which tends to be carried on alone, even when the child is in the company of others. As in parallel play, in which the pre-school child plays beside another child without playing *with* him, so early symbolic play is usually carried on individually, using dolls or a much younger child who passively carries out his role, without really understanding or taking part in it. ("You can be the baby and sleep in the carriage," four-year-old girls will say to a much younger child.) But Piaget traces the way in which this sort of imaginary parallel play evolves into group play with each child taking a different role and reacting to the others involved. The following delightful observation shows clearly how Jacqueline at four was ready for a collective, socialized game, while Lucienne, who was only two, was not.

At 4;7 (12) J. did her utmost to stage a scene with a car ride. L., who was 2;2(18) was in process of constructing a bed, and said "Brr" to show that she was taking part in the movement of the car, but did not stop her own game. What followed was for L. a confused medley of the two games, while J. perseveringly arranged the parts. J. came off victorious, and made L. the wife of a doll, *"You're the wife of this husband. Yes,"* and herself another lady: (J.) *"We're two ladies in a car.* (L.) *Are you in a car, madam?* (J.) *Yes, and I'm throwing your husband and your child through the window* (she threw the doll away)." But L. went and got it and forgot the game.[18]

After the age of seven or eight there is a definite decline in symbolic play, according to Piaget. This age marks the emergence of concrete operations; it also coincides with increased interest in school, and in socialized activities and games with rules. The symbolic games lessen as socialization progresses until by eleven or twelve (period of formal operations) they disappear or are transformed into daydreams (internal) or dramatics (external).

Symbolic play seems to end with childhood; we have seen how the ludic symbols imitate reality ever more closely. As the child accommodates better to the outer world, he has less occasion to assimilate reality to his personal inner needs, thereby distorting it. Accommodation and assimilation, which are increasingly differentiated in the early preoperational period, gradually converge in the years after five until they are once more in equilibrium. For the well-adapted child, play is no longer very different from intellectual activity. Piaget traces this transition from symbolic games to spontaneous creative activity in the play of his son Laurent, who like his sisters created an imaginary village. At about seven, he began to make maps of the country where this village was and to imagine all sorts of people who lived there and the adventures they had. After the age of eight the imaginary characters disappeared, but the careful, detailed maps grew into cartographic models. During an illness that year Laurent worked out descriptions of the climate in different zones of his country, which he called Siwimbal. At nine his interest advanced to real maps of all parts of Europe. Finally, when he was about ten, Laurent's symbolic play appeared on another plane. His maps were quite correct and objective, but the boy now became fascinated with the study of history and reconstructed the costumes, furniture, and architecture of various periods. He dressed tiny toy animals in the costumes of the Middle Ages, the Renaissance, or the eighteenth century. He and a school friend went carefully through the literature on each period so that they could make their reproductions exactly. Here symbolic play began to merge with intellectual and artistic creativity. As Piaget says, "One needs to have seen a little monkey in a wig, a three-cornered hat, silk breeches and lace ruffles, in an eighteenth century setting made of cardboard, in order to understand the pleasure that two eleven-year-old boys can find in spending their leisure time in evoking the spirit of the past."[19] In this description we see clearly how the ludic symbol has developed into "an image whose purpose is no longer assimilation to the ego but adaptation to reality."[20] Laurent's activities no longer represent private fantasy but socialized study. The long period of childhood is at an end.

There is one form, however, in which children's games persist in adult life; that is in the form of games with rules, which Piaget calls "the ludic activity of the socialized being. Just as the symbol replaces mere practice as soon as thought makes its appearance, so the rule replaces the symbol and integrates practice as soon as social relationships are formed."[21] We have already discussed (see Chapter 9) how attitudes toward rules develop. Most rules are handed down from one generation of children to the next, until they become institutionalized. But there is a category which Piaget calls *spontaneous rules,* which may develop out of mere sensory-motor rituals that the child sets up for himself, such as not stepping on lines in the pavement. Or they may be the outcome of symbolic games such as "cops and robbers" which have become socialized, developing simply into chasing games with rules.

Piaget concludes his analysis of children's games with a summary of how games evolve. Practice games grow out of sensory-motor activity and range from mere repetition to chance variations to purposive combinations. If the child begins to arrange blocks according to size and shape, for example, he is passing from mere games to construction, the intermediate step between play and adapted work. If, on the other hand, the child uses blocks to make an imaginary train, his activity is more symbolic than constructive. Symbolic games decline after the age of four, while games with rules increase in interest for children and persist even into adult years. This is because the child, with the help of language, is becoming increasingly socialized, and adapting to the world of reality rather than to the distortions of his own fantasy. These distortions are caused by his original egocentrism, which is only slowly modified, and by his emotional need to work out forbidden feelings. Such feelings may be unconscious or quite openly expressed; in either case, they find outlet in the child's fantasy play and thus help him to adapt to the socializing demands of adult authority. Play, therefore, allows the ego "to assimilate the whole of reality, i.e. to integrate it in order to re-live it, to dominate it, or to compensate for it."[22]

In his theory of play, Piaget goes far beyond the thinking of other authorities in this field. For him play is not just a pre-exercise of the activities a child will need in adult life or an expression of instinctive behavior. Nor is it, as Freud has stated, merely the expression of unfulfilled wishes or subconscious feelings. Symbolic play, says Piaget, "derives essentially from the structure of the child's thought . . . [it is] merely egocentric thought in its pure state."[23] Its sole aim is the free and uninhibited satisfaction of the ego at a period in the child's life when he most needs it. Although Piaget does not so state it, he would probably agree that between the ages of two and four the child is subjected to more parental demands than at any other time in his life. Constantly he hears, "No, no," "Don't touch," "Stay out of the street," "Don't get dirty," "Time for bed." He must be toilet-trained, learn to talk correctly, adapt to a time schedule, and acquire proper table manners. His daily life is polarized around his efforts to adapt to reality and thus please his parents (imitative accommodation) and his efforts to escape from these demands and satisfy his own ego (assimilative symbolic play). As the accommodation to reality becomes easier, the polarity between these two processes decreases. Gradually they converge in increasingly well-adapted functioning, until the child's play becomes almost indistinguishable from his daily reality.

As to the question of whether children believe in their symbolic play, Piaget feels that it depends on the age of the child. While children very early make the distinction between pretense and reality, he says, they refuse to allow the world of adults or of ordinary reality to interfere with the enjoyment of their private reality. It is only after the age of seven that play really becomes make-believe. "The two- to four-year-old child does not consider whether his ludic symbols are real or not. He is aware in a sense that they are not so for others, and makes no serious effort to persuade the adult that they are. But for him it is a question which does not arise, because symbolic play is a direct satisfaction of the ego and has its own kind of belief which is a subjective reality."[24]

One last question remains to be answered. What happens to fantasy, the lovely private world of make-believe, when childhood is left behind? Piaget suggests briefly that some of it is "interiorized" in daydreams and much of it goes to enrich developing intellectual interests, as in Laurent's study of historical periods. He also states, "Creative imagination . . . does not diminish with age, but . . . is gradually reintegrated in intelligence, which is thereby correspondingly broadened."[25]

In this statement Piaget seems to ally himself with cognitive psychologists and those who in recent years have become increasingly concerned with developing creativity in children. Dr. Jerome Singer of the City University of New York believes that fantasy is a creative, constructive skill associated with self-control and the ability to delay gratification and work for long-range goals. His research showed that boys with an active fantasy life could sit still longer than "low-fantasy" boys in a game involving imagining themselves as future astronauts. They also told stories that were rated as more creative than the other boys' stories.[26] Dr. Nina Lieberman of Brooklyn College has published research showing that playful preschool children show more originality of thought than do children who are less flexible and humorous in their play.[27] Dr. David P. Weikart, who has worked out a cognitively oriented curriculum based on Piaget's research, deliberately stresses "sociodramatic play" in the belief that it will help the child to consider the "make-believe" possibilities in his mind, rather than being limited to the toys in his hands.[28] In a study of the fantasy play of primary school children, the author found that her "high-fantasy" group gave many more imaginative details in the stories they told than did the "low-fantasy" children. They were also able to concentrate better on making up stories; and when interrupted, they responded with greater ease and flexibility to the tasks required of them.[29]

Cognitive psychologists are thus beginning to substantiate their belief that make-believe play, the ability to engage in fantasy or daydreaming, is a highly desirable skill closely allied to originality, flexibility, and creative imagination. Teachers and parents, it appears, would do well to follow Piaget's example and encourage ludic play among their children, particularly in the preschool years. Common sense, of course, will dictate boundaries for the adult; he should not be involved in the children's fantasy except in such a way as to make it clear that it *is* fantasy. Since his function is to represent reality to the child, he can good-naturedly apologize for sitting on an imaginary companion by saying, "I'm very sorry, but of course, I couldn't see it!"

12

---

representation

Representation refers, for Piaget, to whatever lies outside the field of immediate perception. This includes whatever was experienced in the past or can be imagined in the future. Memories, images, concepts, and abstract symbols are all included in the realm of representation. In other words, representation in its broadest sense is identical with thought; in a narrower sense it refers to a specific mental image, a copy of reality. Piaget uses the term *representative image* to refer to such a specific memory, whereas the term *symbol* may be linked with what it represents only remotely. We have seen how Jacqueline used her fingers to represent a horse trotting; the only link here was in the drumming movement. Nursery school children who play with water often use it as a substitute for urine, but here the link is more tenuous and often unconscious. The water may become also a symbol of freedom, of the opportunity to indulge in activities forbidden in our toilet-trained society. Thus a host of emotional meanings may accrue to the schema of water, meanings which are highly personal and not shared by all people. This is how a symbol differs from an image; both, together, contribute to the evolution of the broad concept of water.

Piaget feels that concepts develop slowly, from the specific to the abstract. The degree of abstraction possible at any stage in a child's life depends upon the degree of his experience, the amount of meaning he has had a chance to amass around a given symbol. For a child who has seen only one dog, the word "dog" brings to mind only *his* dog, a brown and white beagle named Fido. If he has seen many dogs, he has formed a concept of dogs which includes big and little dogs, fierce and friendly dogs, live and toy dogs, and even pictures of dogs he has never seen. Obviously the formation of such a general concept takes time and experience. The word "dog" is a verbal sign for all of these creatures, but as Piaget points out, the sign may be almost meaningless or it may evoke a whole rich flood of experiences related to dogs. This is why Piaget feels that language is dependent upon the development of symbolism. Imitation gives a concrete image, a picture of dogs immediately experienced. Symbolic play attaches all sorts of related meanings to the term "dog," experiences which are assimilated into the child's consciousness and are suggested by this word. "Dog" finally refers to a whole conceptual schema which has slowly developed around the socially accepted verbal sign. By means of language the world of individual, egocentric experiences can be shared with others; and through this sharing, misconceptions can be corrected and a better adaptation can be made to social and intellectual reality.

The transition from the earliest verbal signs to conceptual schemata comes about slowly and gradually, as shown in the following excerpt:

At 1;1(0) J. used the conventional onomatopoeic sound *tch tch* to indicate a train passing her window, and repeated it each time a train passed, probably after the suggestion had first been made to her. But she afterwards said *tch tch* in two quite distinct types of situation. On the one hand, she used it indiscriminately for any vehicles she saw out of another window, cars, carriages and even a man walking, at 1;1(4). At about 1;1(6) and on the following days any noise from the street, as well as trains produced *tch tch*. But on the other hand, when I played bo-peep, appearing and disappearing without speaking, J. at 1;1(4) also said *tch tch* probably by analogy with the sudden appearance and disappearance of the trains.[1]

Here the sound "tch tch" at first represents a sensory-motor experience, the sound and motion of a passing train. Then other kinds of experience are assimilated to the same verbal sign, so that it assumes a broader meaning which includes any noise, any movement, and any appearing and disappearing. These meanings are private and egocentric; they are related to each other only in Jacqueline's experience and are not shared by the rest of society. Piaget calls these early aggregates of meaning *verbal schemata* and says they are halfway between sensory-motor schemata and conceptual schemata.

The next to develop is the preconcept, which is an intermediate and undifferentiated concept lacking in true generality. Children between two and four, for example, have difficulty distinguishing between the general and the specific, between the class and the individual who is only one of a class. We have described how Jacqueline used to walk with her father along a certain road to watch the slugs. "There it is!" she would cry on seeing one; and when the next one appeared farther on, "There's the slug again!" To her all slugs were "the slug." The same confusion is expressed in the following example:

J. at 3;2(23) could not understand that Lausanne was "all the houses together" because for her it was her grandmother's house "Le Crêt" that was *the Lausanne house*." For instance, talking about a lizard climbing up the wall she said: *"It's climbing up the Lausanne house."* The next day I wanted to see if my explanation had been understood. "What is Lausanne? *It's all these houses* (pointing to all the houses around). *All these houses are Le Crêt.* What's Le Crêt? *It's granny's house, it's Lausanne."* "All these houses" thus constituted a complex object depending on one of its elements which was seen as representing the whole.

Similarly, at 4;2(8), L. did not understand that some pennies removed from a group of pennies formed part of the whole.[2]

This kind of fuzzy, inaccurate thinking is what leads Piaget to call the first half of the preoperational period the *preconceptual stage* (two to four or five years). We have already discussed the magical, animistic, illogical aspects of the child's thought at this age (see Chapter 6). We have seen how symbolic play, which is based on distortion of reality, is at its height in the years from two to four. We have noted the young child's dependence on immediate perception in the conservation experiments (see Chapter 5). Now we see the inability to classify things into related groups and to keep the characteristics of one group separate from those of another. The following is an excellent example of preconceptual reasoning:

At 2;10(8) J. had a temperature and wanted oranges. It was too early in the season for oranges to be in the shops and we tried to explain to her that they were not yet ripe. "They're still green. We can't eat them. They haven't yet got their lovely yellow color." J. seemed to accept this, but a moment later, as she was drinking her camomile tea, she said: *"Camomile isn't green, it's yellow already. . . . Give me some oranges!"* The reasoning here is clear: if the camomile is already yellow, the oranges can also be yellow —a case of "active" analogy or symbolic participation.[3]

In the later half of the preoperational period, however, the child's mind begins to grasp intuitively and uncertainly the relationships of groups and species to each other, and to reason from the part to the whole. Jacqueline at 6;7 was looking for "fuzz-balls" with her father. "They're all called mushrooms, aren't they?" she asked. The following conversation occurred the next day:

At 6;7(9) : *"The crows are afraid of us. They are flying away.—* Yes.—*But the blackbirds aren't afraid.*—No.—*They're the same family, blackbirds and crows, so why are they afraid if they're the same family?"*[4]

Here Jacqueline was reasoning intuitively that what was true of one species of birds should be true of another, regardless of other characteristics. Since both flocks of birds were black, both should have been frightened—an illogical conclusion. Piaget calls this stage (four or five to seven) *intuitive* because it lacks the logical, reversible character of true conceptual thinking. Reasoning is still symbolic, based on personal feelings rather than socialized logic. Piaget quotes Lucienne at 4;10 remarking on an afternoon when she hadn't had a nap, "I haven't had my nap so it isn't afternoon." To her, afternoons were identified irreversibly with naps. No nap meant therefore that it couldn't be afternoon. She was trying to reverse her thinking but was unable to do so correctly because afternoons were to Lucienne still a private symbol rather than a socialized concept.

We have seen this kind of intuitive reaching for the truth in the various stages of indecision and conflict we have observed, whether in the child's understanding of rules or dreams, or his grasp of the conservation experiments. Always we have noted the transitional period, in which the child was not sure whether the clay sausage was the same size or not, whether rules came from God or were decided by men, whether names were an irrevocable part of one or given by one's parents. "Thought at this stage," says Piaget, "continues to be imaged and intuitive, and the equilibrium between assimilation and accommodation is not yet permanent. It is this intuitive thought, semi-reversible but without rigorous compositions, that constitutes the transition from preconcepts to concepts. . . ."[5]

We have seen how, during the intuitive period, the use of symbolic play declines in favor of imitation of real-life activities. This is so because the child is reaching a better balance between assimilation and accommodation, and is more interested in the real world than in his private fantasies. By the age of seven or eight, says Piaget, "there is a real reintegration of play and of imitation in intelligence."[6] Adapted thought reaches a state of permanent equilibrium, ushering in the period of concrete operations. This is possible because of the development of representation. The ludic symbols of earlier childhood tend more and more toward the reality they symbolize; in other words they become more like the representational images developed through imitation. However, they do not become mere carbon copies of reality but are enriched and extended by the child's imaginative experiences in fantasy play. With the establishment of equilibrium between the representations of imitation and the representations of fantasy comes a speeding-up of the thought processes, an ability to range forward and backward in time and space. This, of course, entails reversibility, the ability to retrace one's steps mentally and to think inductively as well as deductively.

The development of language also plays a major part in the transition from representative images to true concepts. As we have already pointed out, it makes possible shared meanings and social intercourse which helps to correct the private distortions of childhood. In fact, according to Piaget, true concepts are not possible without language (a system of signs) and the socialization of meaning that goes with it. The acquisition of these characteristics, and those of increased speed and reversibility described above, complete the transition from preoperational thinking to the higher realm of conceptual thought. "Thus the evolution of thought is shown to be the gradual achievement of equilibrium between assimilation and accommodation through successive stages, while play and imitation evolve correlatively toward their complementary reintegration."[7]

13

---

numbers

Piaget's theories have had their greatest impact upon the teaching of mathematics and science in the elementary school. Particularly in the area of mathematics, the old rote learning methods have left scars for life. There must be thousands of adults today who say, "I never could do math," or "I hated arithmetic and I never understood algebra." But their children come home from the primary grades, talking knowledgeably and even eagerly about sets and Venn diagrams and binary systems. This is the language of the "new math," a revolution in teaching which began in the high schools and in the past ten years has worked its way down to the elementary schools.

Piaget has not been alone in bringing about this revolution. Many professors and scientists, as far back as 1955, helped to spark it, as did the Russians by launching their first Sputnik in

1957. But Piaget has been, says an English mathematician, "the major influence on recent attempts to reconsider the nature of the mathematical experiences provided for children in primary schools."[1] He has brought about a greater concern for concept development and for concrete experience in manipulating materials. For half a century, he has been quietly pointing out that "Knowing is action on objects,"[2] and that lack of experience with concrete materials leads to inadequate mental operations and inadequate development of the abstractions required for more advanced mathematics. Piaget feels that children in the classroom suffer from "cognitive passivity"; they need to take a more active part in discovering facts and relationships. He has shown over and over how sensory-motor structures gradually become internalized to form intellectual structures, that learning must proceed from the concrete to the abstract. So today, instead of chanting $2 + 2 = 4$, $4 + 2 = 6$, $6 + 2 = 8$, first-grade children work with gaily colored wooden rods such as Cuisenaire or the Stern blocks. They play games with the "skipping 2," which shows them in structural form that whenever you add two to a number, the answer is not the next larger number, as in adding one, but skips to the number beyond it: $3 + 2$ is not 4, but 5. Or they learn the structure of odd and even numbers by lining themselves up in pairs, or by placing small blocks in Stern "pattern boards," which show clearly that odd numbers always have one block without a partner.[3] Actively grouping objects into separate classes or arranging them in serial order, children develop an internalized understanding of numbers. They come to realize that numbers can be reversed (by subtraction) or combined (by addition) and that they have the group structure characteristic of the logical groups discussed in Chapter 7 (combinativity, associativity, identity, and reversibility). Thus the construction of number goes along with the construction of logic in the child's mental development; logical operations grow out of simple overt activities such as counting beads, classifying objects, and seriating by length or height.

Piaget feels that, to a remarkable degree, children develop mathematical concepts independently and spontaneously. Parents may spend hours teaching a child to count, but what they are teaching him is mere rote verbalization. Everyone has had the experience of hearing a little child count "one, two, free, five, seven, ten." He knows the names of the numbers, but not what they mean. Teachers who have worked with kindergarten and first-grade youngsters know how long it takes for the concept of number to become established, and how slow and difficult is the process of teaching arithmetic before the structure of number is understood. Piaget implies that there is no sense in rushing this process. The young child can deal only with small numbers, which he can understand intuitively. A three-year-old can count and deal with numbers up to three, a four-year-old up to four, and five-year-old up to five—these are perceptible figures, says Piaget. But "the indefinite series of numbers, and above all the operations of addition (plus its inverse, subtraction) and multiplication (plus its inverse, division), are on the average, accessible only after the age of seven."[4] The reason for this, he points out, is that numbers are both cardinal (1, 2, 3, etc.) and ordinal (1st, 2d, 3d, etc.). This means that children must come to understand that a whole number represents not only a collection of equal units ($3 = 3$ units) but also a position in an ordered series ($3 = 3d$ in a series). It is only after a great deal of concrete experience that the child grasps this dual concept of number and can understand the logic of the indefinite series of numbers. Here Piaget seems to be making a plea for learning by doing. We cannot teach the structure of numbers, he says; we can only create situations in which the child can invent and discover structures for himself.

Before the concept of numbers can develop the child must grasp the principle of conservation of quantity. This, as we have seen, is a logical concept, not a numerical notion. When children realize that quantity is conserved despite changes in appearance, they are ready to accept the fact that the number of objects in a group does not vary, no matter how they are arranged. We have already discussed the experiments with buttons, in which youngsters presented with two equal rows of buttons no longer judged them equal if one row was spread out or pushed close together to change its length. We have also seen that the next step was the development of a one-to-one correspondence between the two rows. Finally, the older children realized that the numbers in each row were the same, however spaced. "Once you know, you know for always," as we have quoted before.

Piaget, in his book *The Child's Conception of Number*, shows how the distinction between cardinal and ordinal numbers grows very gradually out of many experiences of ordering sets of objects in a one-to-one relationship. Such a process is fundamental to the construction of number, since it provides the simplest and most direct measurement of the equivalence of two sets. Piaget had his children match bottles to glasses, by emptying each bottle into a corresponding glass. Then he had them put flowers into vases; only he discovered that some youngsters put more than one flower in a vase! So he switched to eggs and egg cups, and again found the same three stages: the first, in which the sets were not seen as equal; the second, in which there was an intuitive kind of correspondence based on perceptual judgment; and the last, in which the sets were seen as equal in number regardless of changes in grouping.

Lau (6;2) made 6 glasses correspond to 6 bottles. The glasses were then grouped together: "Are they still the same? *Yes, it's the same number of glasses. You've only put them close together, but it's still the same number.* And now, are there more bottles (grouped) or more glasses (spaced out)? *They're still the same. You've only put the bottles close together.*"[5]

Next Piaget posed a problem in which the child had to pick out a number of objects to match a set supplied by the experimenter. He might be shown a row of five beans, or six counters arranged in the form of a hexagon. He would be given a box of beans or counters and told, "Pick out the same number." The younger children would say, "I don't know how many there are," or "I don't know how to do it." The Stage II children would take a guess at the number or construct a figure that looked like the model but usually contained more than six counters. An older child would break up the figures and arrange them in a row which he could match up to his counters. One child, shown a collection of eleven counters, took fourteen out of the box, one or two at a time, and matched them up to eleven. Then he put the last three back. Piaget pointed out that this freedom from perception (the collection of eleven looked much like the pile of fourteen) marked the beginning of operational thinking.

Interestingly, Piaget found that counting aloud had little influence on convincing a child of the equivalence of two sets until he had reached Stage III and already operationally understood equal quantities. "At the point at which correspondence becomes quantifying," he wrote, ". . . counting aloud may no doubt hasten the process of evolution. Our only contention is that the process is not begun by numerals as such."[6]

In these experiments we see that the concept of cardinal numbers grows out of an ordered relationship, one which can be counted. The only way to tell one counter or one bean from another is to put it either before or after the other in time and space. Thus the order of enumeration develops out of the one-to-one correspondence of equivalent sets. But cardinal numbers do not precede ordinal ones, Piaget found. Rather, they develop side by side. When dealing with beans or counters or any other set formed of similar elements, the only thing that distinguishes one element from another is its position. The fourth bean is just like the fifth bean except that it *is* the fourth bean; in fact the beans can be arranged in any order, provided there is an order, so that each bean is counted once and only once.

But when the elements of a set differ in respect to some characteristic such as length or width, they can be arranged in a series determined by that characteristic. In such a case, the ordinal position of each element is important; the smallest element must always be at one end of the series and the largest at the other. Piaget studied the development of this notion of ordinal correspondence by providing ten wooden dolls of clearly differing heights, the tallest being twice the height of the shortest. He also provided ten sticks, varying in size but with less difference between them, to be matched to the dolls. He told each subject that the dolls were going for a walk, and asked him to give each doll the walking stick that belonged to it. Once the two series were arranged to correspond in height, Piaget would reverse or disarrange the sticks and then, randomly picking up a doll, would ask which stick belonged to this particular doll. The child had to have a concept of ordination to be able to match the third longest stick, for instance, with the third tallest doll.

The youngest children, as might be expected, arranged the objects every which way, with no systematic correspondence. Sometimes they matched the tallest or shortest units, but not the rest. Then came progressive intuitive attempts at constructing a series on the basis of perception alone. Finally, the youngsters were able to match up the two series immediately, showing an operational understanding of the correspondence of sizes between them. Piaget noted that there were three ways of going about this. The children might line the dolls up first by height, then line up the sticks, and then put each stick with the corresponding doll. Or they might line up just the dolls, and then pick a stick for each doll, beginning with the smallest, and then the smallest of those remaining, etc. The third way involved just visual judgment; the child would pick up the smallest doll, and then the smallest stick, thus proceeding to build the two series simultaneously, without any previous clues! Here the children were constructing a double asymmetrical series of the type discussed under multiplication of relations (see Chapter 7), which Piaget represented by the following formula:

$$A < B < C < D$$
$$\downarrow \quad \downarrow \quad \downarrow \quad \downarrow$$
$$A_1 < B_1 < C_1 < D_1$$

When the serial order of the sticks was reversed or disarranged, Piaget found that Stage I children were bewildered and chose whatever stick happened to be opposite a given doll. Stage II children tried to discover the correct correspondence by counting, or by perceptually judging the relative sizes. Both of these methods proved inaccurate; when the children counted they consistently made a mistake of one unit. For example, in trying to locate the fifth doll, a child might count the four preceding it, and say, "There are four in front." Then he would count the sticks; 1, 2, 3, 4, and announce that the fourth stick belonged with the fifth doll. Stage III children, of course, had no problems.

Piaget attributed the lack of coordination at Stage II to the fact that ordination was not yet fully operational. Ordination depends on position in a series; when the series was disarranged the child could not reestablish the correct serial correspondence, and thus turned to cardinal correspondence or counting. He was going by the number of the sticks leading to the doll's position, rather than the length of the stick which would correspond to the doll's height.

This confusion between cardinal and ordinal numbers when the series of dolls was disarranged led Piaget to another very interesting experiment. He gave each subject a set of ten sticks of gradually increasing lengths (signified by capital letters A to K; Piaget omits the letter J) and asked him to put them in serial order. When this was done, he gave the child another series of nine sticks (a to i) of lengths which fitted between the sticks of the first series as follows: A a B b C c D d E e F f G g H h I i K. These intermediate sticks were given to the child one at a time, in random order, and he was asked to insert each one in its correct place in the first series. When that was done, Piaget asked him to count the whole series. Depending upon how far he could count without hesitation, Piaget now shortened the series of sticks; if the child stumbled at ten, Piaget left only eight sticks in front of him so that he was confronted with a familiar number that he could cope with.

Figure 11

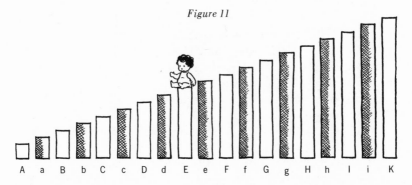

Then Piaget brought out a little doll and told the child to make the doll climb the stairs (represented by the increasing lengths of the sticks). When the doll was on the fifth stair, for example, Piaget would stop the child and ask how many stairs the doll had already climbed and how many he had left to climb. This experiment demonstrated very cleverly whether the child understood the relation of ordinal to cardinal numbers; the doll on the fifth stair must have already climbed four stairs (ordinal position — 1), and must have three stairs left to go (total number of stairs — number of ordinal position). The last step in the experiment was to disarrange the series of sticks and then randomly pick out a stair and ask the same questions— how many came before it and after it?

The results were very enlightening to anyone interested in how children's number concepts develop. The preschool children could not even construct the first series of ten. They could pick out the smallest stick, but "biggest" meant any big stick, independently of its relationship to the other sticks. Another characteristic, which we shall see again in considering the development of time and speed, is that these little children paid attention to only one end of the sticks at a time, so that they constructed a staircase by serializing the tops of the sticks, without regard to the bottoms, or the base line.

Lil (4;0) : "Show me the smallest step. (She pointed to the right one.) Now find one that's a tiny bit bigger than that one. (She picked out a big one and put it next to A.) Show me the biggest. (She pointed at random to a big one without attempting to compare it with others.) Now try to put first the smallest, then one a little bit bigger, then another little bit bigger, and so on. (Lil took I and put it next to A, then E, then H, etc., regardless of order.) We put them like this, look (A, B, C). They make a kind of staircase. Now you go on. (Lil continued with K, F, D, I, G, disregarding the order.) *Like that?*" Having reached this point Lil discovered a procedure, characteristic of this stage, for making a staircase. She took stick B, then stick H, but made the top of B project slightly beyond that of H without paying any attention to the base. She then added K, F, D, I, G, etc., making a series only with the tops. She was then asked to begin again, but with a ruler as base to ensure that the sticks were placed horizontally. She made the series A, C, H, G, E. This was disarranged and the whole staircase constructed and then broken up, and Lil was asked to re-make it. She placed the sticks in the order A, B, C, D, H, F, E, G.[7]

Here we have a fine example of what Piaget calls the "global" approach of the Stage I child. There is no analysis of details or understanding of what the situation calls for—merely a manipulative, sometimes bewildered, attempt to do what the experimenter asks. In the second stage we see what Piaget calls a "perceptual reading of the situation." By trial and error, depending on visual judgment, the child gropes his way toward a correct solution. In the following example we even see "the dawning of relativity"; the child compares stick D with each of the others in order to ascertain its correct relative position. But when it comes to the questions about the doll, he has to re-construct the whole staircase, in order to count how many stairs have been climbed. Like most Stage II children, when asked how many stairs are left to be climbed, he is unable to separate out those already climbed from the total.

San (5;0) : I. He chose correctly the smallest and biggest sticks then arranged A, B, C. When he came to D, he compared it with each of the others in turn, even the biggest, and put it after C. Sticks E–K were then seriated with some trial and error, the cor-rections being made in the series itself.

II. He correctly inserted *i* before K, then compared *e* to E, F, D, E, then to all the others in the row before putting it in position. He did the same with *g*. When he had put *h* before G he cried: *"No, that's not right, it's too difficult."*

III. He counted correctly up to 9. Eight elements were left and he counted them correctly.

IV. The sticks were disarranged and San pointed to steps A, *b* and B as having been climbed when the doll had got to C (for-getting *a*). For the steps preceding D he reconstructed the whole staircase, and for the steps still to be climbed he pointed to the whole series.[8]

Despite the fact that Stage II children can construct the original series, the difficulty that they have with inserting the new elements proves that they are functioning intuitively rather than logically; they are depending on perceptual comparison rather than mental operation. Here is an excellent example of how rigid and unstable is the solution based on perception and intuition, whereas thinking based on logical operations is flexible, reversible, and stable. Piaget points out that sometimes Stage II children can construct a series so efficiently that they seem almost to be operating logically; but when faced with a double series, as in the insertion of a to i, they not only make mistakes but are satisfied with the incorrect results. This, for Piaget, is the proof of the perceptual pudding.

The truly operational child, by contrast, constructs his series with the full understanding that each stick is longer than the one that precedes it and shorter than the one that follows. When faced with the insertion of sticks of intermediate length, he does not regard them as "foreign bodies," but can flexibly assimilate them into his scheme. Most difficult of all, he knows, without counting just how many steps the doll has climbed, because he understands the relationship between the doll's Nth position, and the $N - 1$ steps the doll has already climbed. He knows also that the doll's ordinal position, Nth, corresponds to a cardinal number, N, which can be subtracted from the total (T) number of steps $(T - N)$ to give the number of steps remaining to be climbed. All of this indicates, says Piaget, that "the child has reached a level where both logical and numerical operations are possible."[9]

There are more experiments in this series, and they should be read by every primary teacher. Piaget used cards to form a staircase, with the units marked off on each card just as they are grooved into the Stern blocks, to develop the idea of numbers as consisting of units, each integer one unit greater than the preceding one. To dissociate the ordinal number from the cardinal, he devised a succession of hurdles. Each hurdle required a mat before it and a mat after it, for the jumper to land on. This meant that his subjects had to deal with N mats and $N + 1$ hurdles, in answering questions about the ordinal number (Nth) of each hurdle which required a cardinal number ($N + 1$) of mats. For example, if a child were shown the fourth hurdle and could correctly respond that five mats were required to construct the series to that point (one behind and one in front of each hurdle) he would clearly be able to dissociate ordinal (fourth hurdle) from cardinal (five mats) numbers and to handle both series correctly. The results of these experiments, says Piaget, show "the victory of operation over intuition: in both cases the child coordinates beforehand all the relations involved, because operational composition triumphs over perception, or rather, because the latter is from now on controlled by the former."[10]

Piaget's experiments to illustrate the development of arithmetical processes are similar to the ones we have described under the logical groupings of concrete operations. He discusses the stumbling block presented by problems of part-whole relations, such as in the well-known experiment with brown and white wooden beads (see Chapter 5). He found his youngest subjects so resistant to the realization that the brown beads were also wooden beads that he devised more experiments of this type. As the following example shows, he found it extraordinarily difficult for the young child to understand the inclusion of classes within larger classes; e.g., poppies and bluebells are flowers.

Arl (5;0) : "Look, are there a lot of flowers or a few in this field (a drawing representing 20 poppies and 3 bluebells) ? *A lot.* What color are they? *They're red and blue.* The red ones are poppies and the blue ones are bluebells. *Yes.* I want to make a

very big bunch. Must I pick the flowers or the poppies? *The poppies.* Show me the poppies. (She pointed correctly.) Show me the
flowers. (She made a circular movement to indicate the whole of
the drawing.) Then will the bunch be bigger if I pick the flowers
or the poppies? *If you pick the poppies.* If I pick the poppies, what
will be left? *The bluebells.* And if I pick the bluebells, what will be
left? *The poppies.* And if I pick the flowers, what will be left?
(Reflection.) *Nothing at all.* Then which will be bigger, the bunch
of flowers or the bunch of poppies? *I've told you already.* Think
(repeating the question). *The bunch of poppies will be bigger.* And
what about the bunch of flowers? *It won't be the same.* Will it be
bigger or smaller? *Smaller.* Why? *Because you've made a big
bunch of poppies.*"[11]

Only by trial and error, Piaget found, did Stage II children
discover the correct answer to problems such as this; and it
was not until about seven years of age that they could understand what Piaget calls the additive composition of classes:
$A + A' = B, B - A' = A$.

Piaget drew the distinction here between logical groupings
and mathematical groups. Classes may be grouped inclusively,
but numbers are grouped quantitatively. In other words,
wooden beads may include brown ones, white ones, red, green,
and yellow ones; they all belong to the class of wooden beads.
$A + A' = B$ is not a quantitative relationship; it is simply
inclusive. We have no way of knowing whether A (brown
beads) is greater than A' (white beads). On the other hand,
one dozen brown beads plus one dozen white beads equals
two dozen wooden beads; $A + A = 2A$. This is a precise quantitative relationship.

The addition of numbers produces a new number; this process may be reversed by subtraction. Here we see the properties
of combinativity $(2 + 2 = 4)$ and reversibility $(4 - 2 = 2)$
to which we referred earlier. We also referred to associativity,
the fact that the sum of a series is independent of its order.
Piaget studied children's understanding of this property of

numbers by giving them eight candies, some to be eaten in the morning and some in the afternoon. For the first day Piaget gave out the candy in two piles of four candies (I); for the second day he gave the children seven candies for the morning and one in the afternoon (II). Then he questioned them to see if they understood the equivalence of the two sets.

An (6;11) : "Is there the same amount there (I) and there (II) ? *No. There's 1 there* (II) *and there are 4 there* (I). How many were there before here (II) ? (The two sets of 4 were arranged again, then, before the child's eyes, 3 were taken from the first set and added to the 4 of the second.) Aren't they the same, these (II) and those (I) ? *No. Now there's only 1 here* (II) *and there are 4 here* (I). Could we make them into 4 and 4 again here (II) ? *Yes* (doing so). Will you have the same amount to eat on both days (4 + 4 and 4 + 4) ? *Yes.* And now (changing again to 7 + 1) ? *No, because there are less here* (II)."[12]

This youngster obviously did not conserve the quantity of number even when it was constructed before his eyes. Yet a slightly older child, watching the transformations intently, said in astonishment, "They're both the same!" When Piaget asked, "How did you find out?" he said, "I had a good look, and I saw that you could put three of those [7] here [1]," thus mentally reconstructing the 4 + 4 condition. From this stage it is not far to the logical reasoning of Stage III, which is even capable of correcting its own mistakes:

Laur (7;3) : "Will there be the same amount on both days? *Wait. There* (7 + 1) *they're not arranged the same as here* (4 + 4), *but they're the same, because here* (7) *there are the 3 from there* (1). How many will you eat? *There* (I) *4 and 4, and here, 1 at first and then the 5 others.* Why 5? *Because there are 3 more. Oh no! there are 7 there. There are 8 on both days.*"[13]

In studying the multiplicative relations of numbers, Piaget used a number of the correspondence techniques we have already discussed: relating flowers to vases, eggs to egg cups, etc. For example, he had children put blue flowers in each of ten vases, and then pink flowers in each vase, until they gradually developed the idea of two sets of ten, which could be extended to three or more sets of ten, using the ten vases as the original standard of equivalence. From having to count each set, the youngsters progressed to remembering from one day to the next, "They're the same. . . . I saw yesterday they were the same." Once the sets were seen as equivalent, a given set could be multiplied by any number; three or four or seventeen sets of flowers for the ten vases could be expressed by multiplying 3 or 4 or 17×10. Thus the notion of one-to-one correspondence is implicit in multiplication; the child will sooner or later become aware of multiplication as a way of establishing correspondence between several sets.

As we have seen before and shall see again (see Chapters 16 and 17), whenever the notion of equal units emerges, the concept of measurement is not far behind. Whether it be equal classes ($A = B = C$, which is the same as $A + A + A = 3A$) or equal relations ($A < B < C < D$ by a specified amount X, so that $A + X = B$ and $B + X = C$), once the difference between units is quantified, precise measurement is possible. To illustrate this process, Piaget turned to the various-sized glasses used in the experiments on the conservation of liquid (see Chapter 5). Only this time the child was presented with two or three quantities of colored liquid in two or three containers of different shapes, so that he could not tell by looking at them which glasses contained more, less, or the same. There were some empty containers standing by, and Piaget waited to see how long it would take him to use one of them as a standard measure in discovering a solution to his problem.

As a corollary, the child was given a certain quantity of liquid in a wide, low container and asked to put the same amount into a tall, narrow one. While he experimented with pouring from one vessel to another with his standard container, the child discovered various additive and multiplicative relationships. For example, if the container (C) had to be filled twice to fill a wide low glass (L), then L = 2C. If only one container of liquid filled the tall thin glass (T), then obviously C = T and T = ½L. The solutions of problems such as these involved all the additive and multiplicative operations required to unite parts into a whole, to divide a whole into parts, to coordinate equivalences, and to multiply relationships. At the end of *The Child's Conception of Number*, Piaget points up again the relationships between logical groupings and mathematical groups. All that is necessary to make the multiplication of classes and relations equivalent to the multiplication of numbers is that the differences between classes, and between relations, be equalized. Once this is done, the differences between them, being equal, can be measured, quantified, added, multiplied, and subjected to all the properties of mathematical groups.

As we shall see once more in the studies of time, speed, and geometry, Piaget feels that experiments in child psychology can often throw light on the logical development of scientific concepts. On the basis of the experiments we have been describing, Piaget takes issue with the famous British mathematician Bertrand Russell. According to Russell, he says, the notions of cardinal and ordinal number develop separately; cardinal number derives from the notion of class (a number would be a class made up of equivalent classes), whereas ordinal number develops from the logical relationships of order. But Piaget has shown that very young children make no distinction between cardinal and ordinal number, and that cardinal number as well as ordinal presupposes a relationship of order. His work in this area should be of great interest to all primary teachers.

14

---

the geometry of space

In his study of the child's discovery of spatial relationships—
his "spontaneous geometry"—Piaget points out that the order
of development of geometrical concepts in the child seems to
reverse the order of historical discovery. Euclidean geometry
(concerned with figures, angles, etc.) was developed by the
ancient Egyptians to help them relocate the boundaries of
their fields after the yearly flooding of the Nile. Projective
geometry, dealing with problems of perspective, appeared in
the seventeenth century. Finally, in the nineteenth century,
came topology, the study of spatial relationships and forms
without size or shape. It deals with open and closed figures
such as a simple closed curve which divides a plane into two
regions, one inside the curve and one outside. The plane may
be twisted, stretched, and distorted like a sheet of rubber, so

that squares and triangles lose their shape and become merely rounded polygons. But the distinction between inside and outside, between open and closed figures, is not lost.

Figure 12

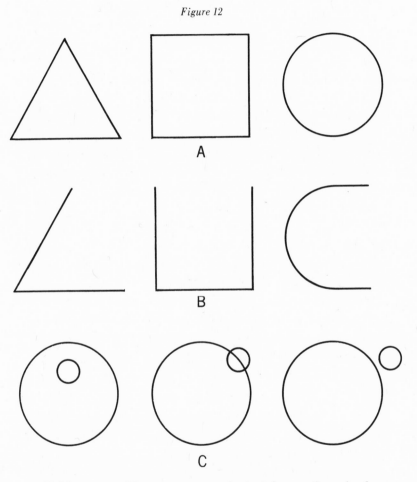

Children, says Piaget, grasp topological figures first. At the age of three a child can distinguish between open and closed figures; if you ask him to copy a square or a triangle he will draw a closed circle (as in Figure 12A). If you show him open figures (as in Figure 12B), he will simply draw open curves. If you give him a circle to copy, with a smaller circle either inside or outside it, or attached to it (as in Figure 12C), he can reproduce this relationship quite adequately. But it is not until he is about five that he begins to draw a square and only later that he can copy accurately the number of sides and angles in a rectangle, as Euclidean geometry requires. According to Piaget, the child begins to develop the notions of Euclidean and projective geometry simultaneously, some time after he has mastered topological relationships. "Curiously enough," writes Piaget, "this psychological order is much closer to modern geometry's order of deductive or axiomatic construction than the historical order of discovery was. It offers another example of the kinship between psychological construction and the logical construction of science itself."[1]

To show how children develop projective constructions, Piaget and his assistants set up little sticks stuck into lumps of modeling clay which they called "fence posts." They set two posts on a table about fifteen inches apart and asked their subjects to place other posts in a straight line between them. A young child would approach the problem from a topological point of view. He would set each post next to the preceding one operating on the basis of proximity rather than by the projection of a straight line. The result was a more or less wavy line connecting the two end posts.

At the intermediate stage children tried to make a straight line by depending on some sort of guide. If the end posts were parallel to the edge of the table they would use that as a guide. But if the end posts were placed diagonally across the table, the task became much more difficult. A child might start off parallel to the edge of the table and then curve around to meet the other end post. But by the age of seven, Piaget found that the average child could build a straight fence consistently in any direction across the table. He would shut one eye and project his angle of vision along the line "as a gardener lines up bean poles." The line was still topological, but the child had grasped the projective relationship.

Piaget became interested in the child's ability to coordinate different perspectives when he took his son Laurent for a ride and realized that the boy did not recognize the familiar mountain he could see from his garden when he looked at it from a different perspective. To study this problem a cardboard range of mountains was constructed which was set on a table between the child and the experimenter. Naturally, each had a different perspective of the mountain range. The child was then given several drawings from which he was asked to select one which showed his own point of view and one which showed the opposite person's view of the mountains. The youngest children, like Laurent, could pick out only the drawing that depicted their own point of view. Even when a child was asked to change places with the experimenter, so that he now saw the mountains from the opposite side, he still could see only his own view; he could not reconstruct the opposite view which had so recently been his! This, says Piaget, is "a clear example of the egocentricity so characteristic of children—the primitive reasoning which prevents them from understanding that there may be more than one point of view."[2]

Similar experiments included standing a doll on a table and then placing a pencil lengthwise, diagonally, or crosswise with respect to the doll's line of vision. The child would be asked to draw the doll's view of the pencil or else to select it from several drawings. The results were much the same; it was not until the age of seven or eight that the doll's angle of vision could be correctly reproduced. Furthermore, said Piaget, it is not until a youngster is nine or ten that he can distinguish between and coordinate different possible perspectives accurately.

At the same time that the child is forming the concept of projective space, he is also learning to construct Euclidean space; the two are interdependent, says Piaget. The conservation of length and of distance are both fundamental to the Euclidean concept of space. We have already discussed experiments on the conservation of length (see Chapter 5), so let us turn to the study of distance.[3] Piaget set two toy trees perhaps two feet apart on a table and asked his subjects whether the trees were near or far apart. Then he put a cardboard screen between the two trees and repeated his question. Most of the younger children felt that the trees were now nearer together; the introduction of the screen seemed intuitively to have cut down the distance between them. One child said the distance was now less, but it would not be if there were a hole in the "wall." So Piaget obliged by cutting a window in the cardboard screen, which caused one child to respond, "They're further, because there's a hole in it." When Piaget then placed a large cube between the trees, the distance immediately seemed lessened.

Stage II subjects also succumbed to the perceptual illusion of lessened distance, particularly with the cube interposed. One said, "It's nearer because it's thicker"; another explained, "It's nearer because it's more full." A third said, "It makes it nearer when you put the brick there . . . because there's less room." For these children, distance is equated with empty space; space occupied by objects doesn't count! Only near the age of seven, said Piaget, do children realize that intervening objects do not change the distance. Thus, the conservation of length and surface is seen to be fundamental to the construction of geometrical concepts, as we have seen that it is in the construction of number.

Once children have acquired the conservation of length, they spontaneously develop the concept of measurement, as we saw also in studying the idea of number. Piaget and his associates studied the development of measurement by means of the following interesting experiment. They showed each child a tower of twelve blocks on a table, and told him to build another tower, of the same height, on a lower table. Plenty of blocks were provided, of different sizes from the model, so that there could be no one-to-one reconstruction of it. There were also sticks and paper strips available to use for measurement should the child so desire, but the rules of the game forbade him to move either tower.

Figure 13

"Children's attempts to deal with the problem," reported Piaget, "go through a fascinating evolution."[4] The four-year-olds, depending on visual comparisons, built their towers to look as tall as the model, often disregarding the difference in the table heights. Given a stick, with the suggestion that they measure, they didn't know how to use it.

Cla (4;1) is given the usual instructions. He spends a long time looking at the model, then carefully makes a tower of his own without looking at the model. When he has finished, he looks back to the model, breaks his up and starts afresh. The same thing happens a third time. "Is yours the same height? *Oh yes.*" He is given a little stick: "You look with that. Can you measure? *I can't use that stick. That one is all right.*" The second stick is a smaller one, and he places this at the top of his tower as an embellishment, saying: *"It's the same height!"*[5]

At a slightly more advanced level, a child might use a long stick to lay across the tops of the two towers—and even if the stick were not horizontal might declare that the two towers were the same. "How can you tell?" Piaget would ask. "Because I've got good eyes!" replied one child.

During Stage II, a child would notice that the tables were of different heights, so that the base of the child's tower was lower. Then he would begin to look around for a way to measure the two towers. Interestingly, the first standard that would come to mind was his own body. The child would put one hand at the base of his tower and one on top, and then walk to the model tower, trying to keep his hands the same distance apart. "Children of about the age of six," remarked Piaget, "often carry out this work in a most assured manner, as if their hands could not change position on the way!"[6] An alternative solution at this age was to measure the height of the tower against the child's own body, and then to walk over to the model tower to compare. Sometimes this led to rather complicated maneuvers, as in the following example:

Dom (6;5) carries bricks to the model to compare their size. When he has finished he puts one hand over the top of the model and the other against its base. He keeps his hands at this distance and so transfers the height to his copy. Still not satisfied, he goes back to the model and climbs on to a chair: *"I'm not big enough. I got to be the same height to see properly."* He uses his own body as a yardstick, putting one finger against himself at the level of the base and joining his head and the top with a ruler. He then goes across to the other tower and repeats this maneuver: "Could you do it another way? *I could use my arm* (holding it against the two towers in turn). What about this brick?" (He holds the brick at the level of the base of one of the towers, and holding one hand aloft, he transfers this height to the other tower.) [7]

Piaget calls these two approaches "manual transfer" and "body transfer." They illustrate a first step toward conservation of length, measured with the nearest and most familiar tool of the child—his own body. One little boy simply climbed up on a chair and hugged his tower to see how high it came on him. Then he went over to the model and did the same thing. Other children went through various movements, spreading their fingers or marking their legs. As they realized the unreliability of these measures they looked around for a symbolic object, and turned to blocks, sticks, or strips of paper. One boy even built a third tower right next to the model, and then carried the blocks over to the lower table and rebuilt it as a standard for his tower. Here we see the beginnings of logical reasoning. If A (the model tower) = B (the movable tower), and C (the child's tower) = B, then A = C.

The first stages in the evolution of measurement involved the use of rulers in different ways. First the child would use a ruler only if it was the same height as the tower. Then he learned to use a longer one and mark the height of the tower with his finger. One child was even able to take account of the angles of rulers sloping from tower top to tower top, and from base to base, and judge that if the rulers were parallel, the heights were the same.

Lau (6;1) merely looks at the model to begin with but soon finds this difficult owing to the difference in base levels. He carries bricks across to compare them more closely, and later stretches his arms to span the tops of the towers. But he goes on to say, *"The table comes this high,"* showing the point on the model corresponding with the base level of the copy. He now stands against his tower and looks for a reference point on his own body (his shoulders) but thinks better of it and finds a ruler to measure the two towers. He succeeds because the ruler happens to be the same length as the towers. When asked to measure with a longer ruler, he judges the difference by eye and loses his reference point in the process. He therefore bridges the tops and uses another ruler to bridge the bases, noting that the rulers are parallel: *"It's the same height because they slope the same."* When given a shorter ruler he measures his tower and uses his own hand to make up the difference.[8]

The final step came when the child realized that he could use a rod shorter than the tower, and by repeated applications, measure the height of the tower. This discovery involved two new operations of logic: the division of the tower into parts such that part A = part B = part C; and the displacement of these parts onto the second tower to build a system of units. Thus A = B = C, being three equal units, became A + A + A = 3A, marking the birth of true measurement.

To study the construction of space in two dimensions, Piaget presented his subjects with two sheets of white paper, one of which had a red dot on it about halfway between the center and the corner on the upper right-hand side. Each child was asked to locate a dot on the blank sheet in exactly the same place. Rulers, strings, and other guides were provided. The youngest children ignored them and just took a guess, using visual approximation. Children at Stage II would measure either from the top down or from the side over, and were surprised that this one measurement did not give them the correct position! Then they tried to measure from the corner of the paper, keeping their rulers at the same slant. Finally, at about eight or nine, the youngsters realized that a coordination of two measurements was required ". . . to know where to put the point, in this direction and in that one, too."[9] They had grasped the idea that measurement in two dimensions establishes the axis of coordinates—a central idea of Euclidean space.

Only one more of these geometrical experiments will be described here, although many others can be found in *The Child's Conception of Geometry* by Piaget, Inhelder, and Szeminska. This is the well-known "Cows on the Farm," designed to study the conservation of area and how it is measured. It is based on the Euclidean axiom, "If two equal parts are taken from two equal wholes, the remainders will also be equal." To illustrate this, Piaget and his co-workers produced

Figure 14

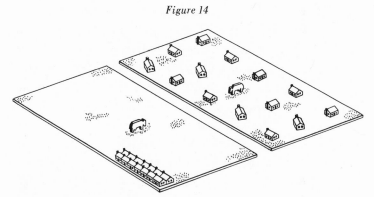

Figure adapted from Piaget, Inhelder, and Szeminska, *The Child's Conception of Geometry*, p. 262.

two identical sheets of green cardboard representing two farmyards. Each farmyard had a little wooden cow placed on it, and the subjects were asked whether the cows had the same amount of green grass to eat. When this was established, the experimenter produced a little farmhouse (wooden cube) for one farmyard, and explained that the farmer needed a place to live. Would the two cows still have the same amount of space for grass? Even the youngest subjects would agree that the farmyard with no house provided more space for the cow to graze. Then a house was produced for the second farmyard, and again the cows had the same amount of grassy space. "The necessary character of Euclid's axiom," wrote Piaget, "seems to be evident at all ages."[10]

Then Piaget kept adding more and more farmhouses, one on each piece of land, and repeating the question. The difference was, however, that on one farm the houses were all placed side by side to form a compact row, whereas on the other they were scattered all over the farmyard, giving it a very cluttered look. Piaget was interested in seeing at what point the children would succumb to the perceptual configuration and declare that the more open-looking farmyard contained more grassy space. Some children would stick to the logical axiom up to fourteen pairs of houses and suddenly fail on the fifteenth, because the appearance of more grassy land in the open farmyard was "somehow irresistible." The children who could hold out against the perceptual appearance of the scattered houses on logical grounds were usually about seven and a half. The younger ones relied on perception, and beyond that intuitively felt that the two *should* be equal, but could not bring themselves to admit it when the farmyards appeared so different.

Here we have an interesting example of a conservation problem in reverse. It again illustrates how fundamental to all mathematical and scientific thought is the basic notion of conservation. Piaget, through his experiments, has brought forth many unexpected revelations about the development of mathematical concepts and of human knowledge in general.

15

perception and learning

If Piaget's major interest is cognition, his "minor" (to quote Flavell) is perception. Since about 1940, he and his co-workers have been reporting regularly on their research in this field; by now there have been almost fifty journal articles published in French. These have been summed up in one imposing volume which was recently published in English, *The Mechanisms of Perception*. The experiments described here are taken from it, but the writer is indebted to Flavell and Baldwin for much of the theoretical explanation.

Perception is a subject which has interested scientists and philosophers as far back as Descartes. There have been many schools of thought, from the eighteenth-century associationists, such as Hume and Locke, to the modern "transactionalists," for whom perception involves a transaction between the perceiver and the setting in which the stimulus is perceived. Basically the major controversy is between nativism and empiricism. The nativist school believes that perception is innate and immediately given. We see things as they look to us because that's the way they are. The empiricists argue that we learn through sensory experience to see things and that we see them as we expect or wish them to be. To counter the nativist position, they cite optical illusions such as the familiar

Figure 15

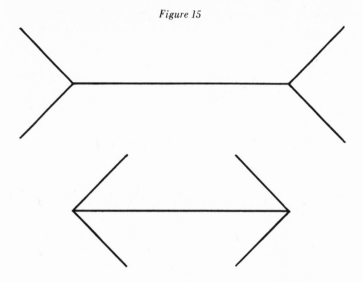

Müller-Lyer illusion, in which two lines are of equal length but appear to be unequal. Ames, in a famous experiment to show how experience affects our perception, constructed what looks like a rectangular window moving back and forth.[1] (See Figure 16.) Actually it is a trapezoid with one end much longer than the other, which makes it look the way a rectangle looks in perspective. Moreover, the whole "window" is rotating, but since the front end (A) is longer, it always appears nearer than the back end (B), and thus is seen as moving back and forth closer to the observer than b. Experiments such as this draw attention to the fact that we see what we expect to see—what we have experienced before and therefore are familiar with.

Piaget accounted for the innate-versus-acquired problem by distinguishing between *perception*, which is the quick, immediate view of the stimulus one gets at first glance, and *perceptual activity*, which involves experience, judgment, and correction of distorted first impressions. Both are involved in

Figure 16

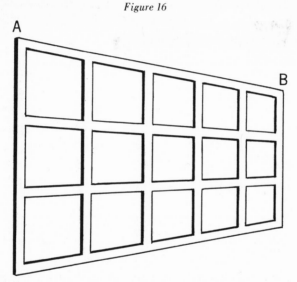

the perceptual act, which consists of a series of encounters. Piaget's theory of encounters is based on a probability model. If one were to look at a picture with 100 details (encounterable elements) in it, he might perceive half of them at the first brief encounter, leaving 50 elements unnoticed. On the second encounter, he would focus on half of the remaining elements, leaving 25 unnoticed. On the third encounter, he would perceive half of the 25, or 12½, and so on, until all encounterable elements had been observed. Thus the rate of encounters per microinterval would be represented by a curve that levels off by gradually decreasing amounts—50 of the elements sampled on the first encounter, 75 (50 + 25) on the second, 87½ (75 + 12½) on the third, and so forth.

Piaget does not define exactly what an encounter is (perhaps a micro-movement of the eyes),[2] but he advances this theory because it explains several kinds of phenomena. For one thing, it accounts for error in perception. A lot of details may be overlooked in a hasty first encounter; the eye tends to fixate or *center*, to use Piaget's term, on only the most compelling elements. This leads to a distorted perception, which must then be gradually corrected by *decentering*. During subsequent encounters the eye has time to fixate different parts of the stimulus and visually explore all its elements. Mistaken impressions are corrected as the multiple encounters are compared and integrated; thus distortion is replaced by accuracy of perception.

Decentering assumes a very important position in Piaget's theory, both perceptually and intellectually. We have seen in the conservation experiments how centering on the length of the clay and not the width brought about errors in judgment. In the study of number we have seen how children constructed a staircase by centering only on the tops of sticks or cards, without regard for keeping a consistent baseline. Decentration provides correction and regulation, leading to equilibrium. Centration leads to errors.

The reason for this, according to Piaget, is that objects seen in space are not all equally well perceived. Suppose the stimulus is a line; if it is encountered only briefly (e.g., flashed on a screen for a fraction of a second), it is seen as shorter than a line of the same length presented in full exposure. If the line appears directly before the eyes, it stimulates the center of the retina, and appears longer than one which is on the periphery of the visual field. The duration of the exposure time, the clarity of the lighting in which the line is seen, its distance from the eyes, and the degree of attention with which the observer focuses upon it—all of these factors contribute to a tendency to overestimate or underestimate. A line seen at the center of the visual field, fully exposed in clear light, by an attentive observer is perceived as longer than it really is. Piaget calls this *elementary error I:* overestimation owing to centration.

Another related error to which centration leads is the "error of the standard" (*elementary error II*). This arises when a subject is asked to compare objects, one of which is left in place (the standard) while the others are presented one at a time. "The standard is systematically overestimated," Piaget explains, "just because it plays a privileged role in the comparison."[3] The subject keeps returning to the standard to make his judgments, thereby centering it much more often.

An experiment conducted with Marc Lambercier, an associate of Piaget's, demonstrated these findings clearly. The subjects, including both children and adults, were asked to make a comparison between a standard vertical rod and a number of other rods, ranging from shorter to longer than the standard. They were asked, "Is this one [the variable] shorter or longer than this one [the standard], or is it equal to it?" When the two rods were close together (i.e., in the center of the retina), the standard was underestimated. But as the distance between them was increased, the standard was consistently overestimated. Piaget's explanation for this is that "the subject, being forced constantly to return to the standard in order to make his comparison at greater distances of separation, centered it more frequently, or for a longer time, or more attentively, etc., and by this very fact came to overestimate it.

At smaller distances, on the other hand (smaller for children than for adults), the subject, having both the standard and the variable constantly in view at the same time, and being familiar with the standard which he did not in any case have to lose sight of, preferentially centered the variable and thus over-estimated it."[4] He found support for his hypothesis in the results of two variations in the experimental procedure. If the standard and the variable were both removed at the same time, and the standard was then replaced without the subject's knowing that it was the same standard, he was less likely to overestimate it. Also, if the instructions were reworded so that the variable became the standard of comparison, and the subject was asked to compare the previous standard with the variable, it often happened that the variable then became the one that was overestimated!

Piaget became very much interested in this question of the relationship between comparison figures and set himself to work out the following problem: why, if A is less than B, is B perceived as larger when accompanied by A than when perceived alone? He expressed this as $B(A) > B$; or B in relation to A is greater than B by itself. In his characteristically rigorous way, Piaget then set himself to study at least a dozen well-known visual illusions and express his findings in a mathematical formula that would predict the size of the error that could be expected in relation to the changing values of elements in the perceptible situation—the length of lines, the distance between stimuli, the age of the subjects, etc. In the case of the Müller-Lyer illusion, the error of estimation of length was found to vary predictably with the length of the barbs on the ends of the equal lines, and the size of the angles formed by the barbs with those lines. Piaget called his formulation *the law of relative centrations*; it represents, as Flavell says, "the high-water mark of quantification in Piaget's theoretical system."[5] The contrast between the precise, carefully controlled, statistically reported experiments in perception and Piaget's unstandardized clinical approach to the study of intelligence is nowhere more clearly evident. However, since the explanation of these experiments is highly technical and requires a specialized background in the field of perception, we will turn from them to a consideration of the relationship between perception and intelligence.

Piaget feels that perception and intelligence evolve independently of each other; that intelligence is continually developing, whereas perception shows no such development but rather is "enriched" by the emerging structures of intelligence. To illustrate this, he describes an experiment which points up the difference between perception and conception.[6] As part of the investigation of a constant error arising in the comparison of the length of two parallel lines, two lines of equal length were presented, one set to the left of the other, as in Figure 17.

Figure 17

The subjects were children of five, eight, and eleven, as well as adults. It was found that five-year-old children were less subject to perceptual illusion than their elders. They tended to judge the displaced line as being only slightly longer, whereas eight-year-olds made the maximum error in judgment. The error was less for eleven-year-olds and even less than that for adults; but the five-year-olds performed considerably better than adults. Piaget explains that the younger children have not yet learned to structure their perceptual space in terms of the natural coordinate axes; this Euclidean notion of space does not develop until the age of concrete operations (see Chapter

14). Older children, used to thinking in terms of verticals and horizontals, overestimate the line which is displaced horizontally.

In contrast to this perceptual task, Piaget describes a conservation experiment in which two rods of equal length were presented first, with the subjects agreeing that they were equal.[7] When one rod was projected ahead of the other, however, the younger children reported that it was longer because it "reached farther." The Stage II children wavered back and forth between the uneven appearance of the lines and their demonstrated equality. But by the age of seven, the subjects were certain that the lines were equal in length, not because they looked the same, but because they *were* the same.

The juxtaposition of these two experiments points up very clearly the difference between perception and conception (or operations). Perception depends upon immediate experience and is subject to error. Conception depends on thought, which can go back in time to the point at which the two rods were seen to be equal and form a judgment strong enough to overcome the perceptual illusion.

While perception is less stable and dependable than the structures of intelligence, Piaget believes that through perceptual activity children do learn to correct distortions and compensate for illusions. The child of two can recognize his toys from any perspective, even though he may not *conceptually* realize that things look different from different points of view. In fact, during the preoperational years, a child's perceptual activity is better adapted to the real world than is his thinking. We have seen that the young child's thought is magical, illogical, animistic, and based on intuition rather than reality. He believes that the moon follows him around, that clouds move in order to bring the night, and that mountains grow because stones have been planted. In spite of all these misconceptions, the preschooler can find his way around the neighborhood and operate very realistically in a world of constantly changing perceptions. Colors look different against different backgrounds, people look smaller when they are a block away, and objects look different when they are upside down or inside out. Yet the little child soon learns to cope with these changing impressions of constant objects by developing what is called *perceptual constancy.*

This means that we learn to perceive sizes and shapes and colors as they are, even when we see them from angles and perspectives that make them look distorted. Just as the baby learns that objects exist constantly even when they are out of sight, so the preschooler learns that Daddy is still six feet tall, even when he is a block away and looks smaller. Perceptual constancy sets the stage for conservation, which is really constancy of quantity, number, weight, etc., despite changes in form. But conservation depends on thought and therefore is of a higher order than perceptual activity of any kind. "Perception is not, therefore, the source of knowledge," writes Piaget, "because knowledge derives from the operative schemes of action as a whole. Perceptions function as connectors which establish constant and local contacts between actions or operations on the one hand, and objects or events on the other."[8]

Thus Piaget makes it quite clear that structurally and functionally, perception is subordinate to intelligence. Perception gives us direct knowledge of the world around us, but it is subject to error. Perception corrects itself through decentration, but it is not reversible, as is thought. Perception transmits messages describing the world as it is seen, but intelligence decodes them. Perception at its best never goes beyond the level of preoperational thought, and as such is immediate, intuitive, and sometimes wrong.

What Piaget is really rejecting here is the position of the

Gestalt psychologists, who have dominated the field of perception since the thirties. They argue that the laws of organization, of figure-ground discrimination and perceptual constancy, are innate and immediate, whereas Piaget has shown that they are acquired gradually through sensory-motor experience. He is not alone in this; there are a number of American psychologists,[9] whose research supports a developmental view of perception. The importance of their work, and of Piaget's, is that it helps parents and teachers to understand the learning problems of children. If, as Piaget shows, there are systematic distortions in children's perception such as *the error of the standard*, we begin to understand why young children may have difficulty in copying letters from the board or recognizing the same word in different typefaces. As adults, our perception is so highly developed, through years of perceptual activity, that we forget that a page of print does not look to children as it does to us. Children tend to center on certain words and not see the rest of the sentence, whereas our decentered vision takes in a whole line in one sweep of the eyes. Now, thanks to Piaget, we have a rationale and a sequence of experiences to help us correct children's inadequacies and give them a more mature approach to learning.

In fact, perceptual-motor training is presently very much in vogue in this country. It has arisen from a different rationale; Hans Werner at Clark University, who influenced Alfred Strauss and Newell Kephart, was really the source of this movement. Nevertheless, Piaget's theory of development has given new depth and meaning to this approach and supplied a comprehensive theoretical framework into which it fits. Stated very briefly, the purpose of perceptual-motor training is to make up for any observed deficits in perception or motor coordination in children who have learning disabilities. To quote Dr. Gloria Wolinsky of Hunter College,

It might be said that possibly what is seen in the behavioral activity of a brain-injured child is the activity of a child who has not completed the sensory-motor stage in certain areas and who is attempting to build acts of intelligence on a structure that is not yet free of the demands of the sensory-motor period.[10]

In such a case, what is needed is more experience at the sensory-motor level in order to develop the necessary perceptual processes. Piaget says that "perception renders indispensable services to sensory-motor activity, but that it is reciprocally enriched by this activity. . . . [For example] the size of an object is variable to the sight but constant to the touch . . . the whole sensory-motor development imposes a coordination between the visual and the tactilo-kinaesthetic sensations."[11]

If a child is not succeeding in the activities generally expected of kindergarten or first-grade children, the teacher well versed in Piagetian theory can take a careful look at him and see at what developmental level he *is* operating. Perhaps he cannot copy letters from the board like other children. She might give him a sheet of paper and ask him to draw a circle or a square for her. If he does not know how, she might present him with models and ask him to copy them. If he can produce only a lopsided circle or a square with "ears" for corners instead of sharp angles, she goes back to an earlier level of development and gives him experience with handling and copying forms at a gross motor level. She might give him form boards into which he can fit large circles, squares, and triangles after he has felt them and observed their distinctive characteristics. Or she might ask him to go to the board and draw big round circles with chalk until he has the feeling of a circle in his muscles as well as an image in his mind.

Once the child has a kinesthetic and tactile as well as a visual image of a circle, the teacher might begin to scale down his reproductions. She might give him plastic templates to trace inside of, or put lines on the board to limit the size of his circles. Eventually. her goal would be to have him copying circles from the board on paper at his seat. Then by adding lines in the right relationships to the circle, the child could begin successfully to reproduce letters such as *a*, *b*, or *p*.

There are many ways in which sensitive teachers can observe and provide for deficiencies in children's experience. Perhaps the child has trouble with auditory discrimination—he can't hear the difference between *cap* and *cat*. This will give him problems in learning to read and spell. The teacher may expose him to high and low tones, different kinds of musical instruments, and all sorts of listening games, which will help to fill in the gap in the child's experience before it creates problems for him. In other words, teachers are becoming increasingly adept at "prescriptive teaching"—pinpointing a child's deficits and providing perceptual activities especially selected to help him overcome them.

This kind of training also gives many kinds of concrete experience from which a child gradually learns to generalize. For example, a teacher trying to develop the concepts of "same" and "different" might line up two boys and one girl and ask the class which one was different. Or she might choose three boys and have one facing the blackboard while two faced the class. She might have children put chairs in a row, but have one chair faced in a *different* direction. She might make a pile of four blocks and ask a child to make one using the *same* number of blocks. There are a thousand and one ways in which a capable teacher can feed experiences to a child from which he can generalize an abstract concept needed at his particular level of intellectual functioning, beginning with his own body and extending out into the world around him.

This brings us to the problem of timing or, as J. McV. Hunt[12] calls it, the problem of "match." We must learn to match our teaching to the child's level of development, whether it be at the preschool level of perceptual training or at more advanced levels of curriculum. If we teach at a level below the child's stage of development, he is bored because it is too easy for him. If our teaching is over his head, the child is frustrated and confused. But if it is geared to the child's operational level, then it can present him with just enough "cognitive conflict" to stimulate and interest him. Thus learning and educational experiences must be kept in equilibrium with the child's level of development. As F. H. Hooper puts it in a recent paper, he must have "the right kind of experience at the right time."[13] We need a great deal more research in order to know precisely what to teach when, and how best to fit our teaching to the individual child. But we are making progress, and it is indicative of the genius of Piaget that his theories are finding applications in special education as well as among normal children.

16

---

time

It is an interesting fact that Piaget's studies of time and speed were suggested by Albert Einstein, author of the theory of relativity. At a symposium on the philosophy of science in 1928, Einstein, who was the chairman, became very much interested in Piaget's report of his experiments on the thinking of children. He stimulated Piaget to look into the relationship between time and speed in children's thinking, to see which came first, how they were related, and how one depended on the other. In Einstein's theory of relativity, time and space are relative to the speed of light. In physics, however, time is measured by speed, and speed is defined by time, which sets up a vicious circle. In an effort to discover how these concepts develop in children, Piaget devised experiments to study all aspects of this complex relationship. He published his results in two volumes that have only recently been translated into English: *The Child's Conception of Time* and *The Child's Conception of Movement and Speed.*

The concept of time, says Piaget, "is constructed little by little, and invokes the elaboration of a system of relations."[1] The baby's first temporal experience is probably a vague feeling of duration; he may be waiting for his bottle and becoming aware of the waiting because he is hungry. Soon he learns that events take place in sequence; when Mother comes into the room, the bottle appears soon afterward. So the child learns to expect a series of events in before-and-after sequence. Many parents have noticed that the hungry infant will stop crying when he hears his mother in the kitchen. This indicates that he anticipates being fed very shortly. When the baby is approximately a year old, if Mother hides his bottle under a pillow he will look for it. In other words, he is remembering that the bottle is there even when it is out of sight. This act indicates not only that object constancy has been achieved but also that the baby is recalling an event which took place earlier in time.

But Piaget noticed a curious thing. He was watching his thirteen-month-old nephew chasing a ball one day. It rolled under an armchair and he was able to retrieve it. Then it rolled under a sofa where he couldn't see it—and the toddler ran back and looked under the armchair! Piaget tested this out experimentally and found that if he hid a toy under one cushion and then very slowly, with the child watching, hid it under another cushion, the children younger than a year old would look for the toy under the first cushion. After about three weeks of this, the children learned to go to the second cushion first, but if they didn't find the toy immediately, they went back to the first cushion. It was not until much later that the children searched only under the second cushion. Piaget explained this by saying that a baby's perception of time—the order in which perceived phenomena occur—is subjective and inaccurate. Babies are "not yet capable of reconstructing the history of external phenomena themselves."[2] By this he meant that a child proceeds rigidly to act out what he has seen in the order in which he ex-

Figure 18

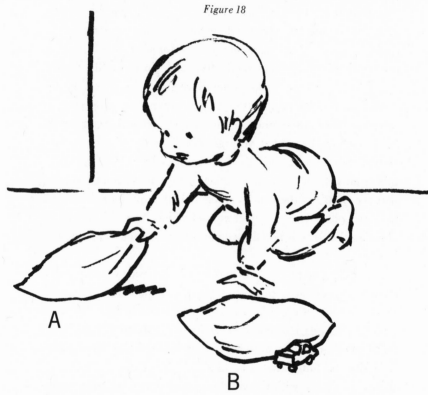

A

B

perienced the events. He goes to the first place he saw the toy because that is first in his time sequence—and probably forgets the rest of the series of events. He does not have the flexibility of thought to skip the first cushion and go to the second one until he is older.

But as the child grows, capacity to retain events in memory

increases steadily and is extended to ever more remote happenings. Jacqueline, before she was two, could remember events from two days before, as the following observation shows.

1;7(27): Jacqueline, on the terrace of a mountain chalet, locates the people I name, taking into account their recent displacement. "Where is Mother?" She points to the chalet. "Where is Grandpa?" She points down to the plain where her grandfather went two days before. "Where is the boy?" She points to the chalet. "Where is Vivianne?" She points to the woods where Vivianne went for a walk.[3]

In the sensory-motor period, the child has learned to order his temporal schema in relation to that of external things. By the time he is two he is aware of the sequence of events and of the duration of intervals ("It's time for dinner" or "time for bed") in a practical sort of way. But his thinking is still egocentric and centered on his own needs and desires, as Piaget discovered when he began to question four- and five-year-olds about their age. He found that children tend to confuse age with height. The one who is bigger is the elder, regardless of birth order. This has been noticed by many kindergarten and first-grade teachers whose pupils ask them about their "fathers." Usually these are visiting husbands, but at least once for me my "father" was a tall college-age son who came to help with a Christmas play! This confusion of generations comes about, says Piaget, because the child's idea of aging is static and discontinuous; "when growing stops, time apparently ceases to operate."[4] He found that young children didn't know who was born first, their grannies or their mothers, and frequently insisted that they were there when parents or older siblings were born, as in the following interview:

Bor (4;9): *"I have two brothers, Philippe and Robert.* Are they older or younger than you? *Older than me.* Much older? *Yes.* How old are they? *I don't know.* Do they go to the big school?

Yes, both of them. Is one older than the other? *No, both of them are the same age* (wrong). Were they born on the same day? *Yes* (wrong). Are they twins? *No.* But they are the same age all the same? *Yes, the same age as myself.* Who was born first then? *Philippe and then Robert* (correct). Who was born first, Philippe or you? *I* (wrong). So who is the oldest of you three? *Nobody.* You told me you were born before Philippe, so you must have been there when Philippe was born? *Oh sure, I was there* (this seems quite evident to him . . .). Who was born first in your whole family? *No one. Philippe came second, then Robert, and I was the fourth because I am four years old."*[5]

Piaget attributes such incomprehensible reasoning to the child's egocentric conception of time, which confuses objective reality with subjective intuition. From the child's point of view, the existence of others begins in his own memory; before he was there they were not there either. Also a child accepts others as he sees them, with no conception that they were ever once young. One little boy told Piaget that his grandfather was born "old right away." Moreover, since age is equated with size, those who have stopped growing, such as mothers and grandmothers, are often considered the same age or not aging any more because they are "old already." On the other hand, the child who is growing sees himself as able to overtake his forebears and even to catch up with older siblings. A youngster of four and a half confided to Piaget that he had a brother two years older, but he expected to catch up with him "if I eat a lot of soup."

Piaget then describes an intermediate stage in which the child grasps the notions of succession or duration but cannot coordinate the two. In the first case, he may know that his father is older than his mother because he was born first, but does not realize that he continues to remain older. Or he may be aware that age differences persist but be unable to tell in what order people were born, as in the following example:

Dour (7;5): "How old are you? *7½.* Have you any brothers or sisters? *No.* Any friends? *Yes, Gerald.* Is he older or younger than you? *A little older, he's 12 years old.* How much older is he than you? *Five years.* Was he born before or after you? *I don't know.* But think about it, haven't you just told me his age? Was he born before or after you? *He didn't tell me.* But is there no way of finding out whether he was born before or after you? *I could ask him.* But couldn't you tell without asking? *No.* When Gerald will be a father, will he be older or younger than you? *Older.* By how much? *By five years.* Are you getting old as quickly as each other? *Yes.* When you will be an old man what will he be? *A grandfather.* Will he be the same age as you? *No, I'll be five years less.* And when you will be very, very old, will there still be the same difference? *Yes, always.*"[6]

Finally, as children reach the operational level, at seven to eight years old, they begin to coordinate the notions of succession and duration, and separate the idea of age from that of size.

Pol (8;3): *"I have two small brothers, Charles and Jean.* Who was born first? *Me, then Charlie and finally Jean.* When you are grown up, how old will you all be? *I'll be the oldest, then Charlie and then Jean.* How much older will you be? *The same as now.* Why? *It's always the same. It all depends on when one was born.*"[7]

Piaget says that before the operational stage, thought is not reversible, and therefore the youngster cannot conceive of his parents as having had a past. His understanding of age is based on the obvious perceptual characteristic of size; one is bigger so he must be older. Gradually he develops a primitive intuitive approach, often confused in some aspects, until finally he is capable of reaching an equilibrium among all the factors involved in age and even projecting into the past or the future. These are the familiar three stages that we have met several times before.

Piaget then went on to study more carefully the relationship between age and rate of growth. He presented drawings of an

apple and a pear tree that were planted a year apart. At first
the apple tree was larger; then the two were the same; but by
its fifth year the younger pear tree had surpassed the apple tree
in size. This meant that in arranging the drawings the child
had to take into account the increasing size of each tree, and
then relate the growth of the two trees to each other, with the

Figure 19

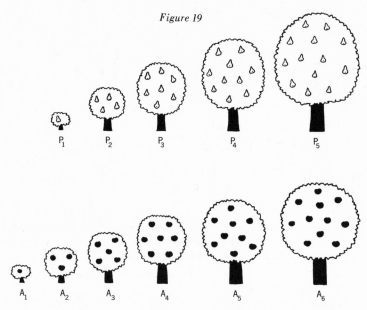

pear tree always a year behind in age. The child was thus
forced to dissociate age from height in answering Piaget's
questions about which tree was older during a particular year.
The first three years presented no problem, but when the pear
tree became larger than the apple tree, the same difficulties
arose. The younger children insisted the pear tree was now
older because it was bigger; the children in Stage II vacillated
and hesitated between the apple tree which was planted first
and the pear tree which was bigger. Finally, in the seven-to-
nine age group, one child answered, "The apple tree is always

older because it was planted first. The pear tree grows more quickly, but the apple tree is older."[8] Thus, time became divorced from size and acquired "a special structure based on the systematic correlation of durations (ages) and the succession of events (births and anniversaries)."[9]

Piaget found it significant that young children based their judgments of people's ages not on inner criteria (such as that adults know more) but on external characteristics such as size. He therefore proceeded to study introspective estimates of time, based on metronome tests, on fast or slow raps on a table, and on having a child draw quickly or slowly for 15 seconds. Almost invariably, he found that younger children thought that quick work must take longer than slow work. A child of four insisted it took him longer to make the rapid drawings because "it went faster when I worked more quickly . . . it took more time."[10] The children here seemed to be relying on the results achieved: more strokes or raps = more time consumed. It was not until they reached more advanced ages that they were able to judge time separately from action. They had to be able to evaluate the length of time that had passed, regardless of how fast they worked. Children above seven said, "I was working more quickly but it took the same time," or "I went more slowly, but I rather think it took the same time."[11]

In other words, the concept of time is dependent on the order of succession of events and on the duration of time intervals; these are two distinct and fundamental systems which must be coordinated. In order to study each one separately, Piaget devised brilliantly simple experiments, some of which will be described here. To study the succession of events, he presented his subjects with two flasks; one an inverted pear-shaped glass (I) with a tap controlling the flow of water into a cylindrical glass (II) underneath it. Piaget would let fixed quantities of colored water run out of I into II so that as the water level fell a certain interval in I, it would rise a corresponding interval in II. Then he gave his watching subjects several sheets of paper on which the apparatus was drawn and had them color in the water levels in the two glasses as they appeared at each successive interval until I was empty and II was full.

Figure 20

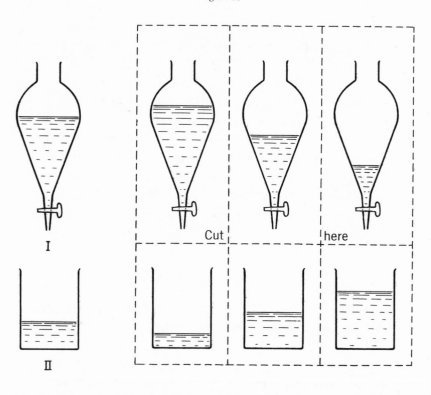

The next step in the experimental procedure was to mix up the drawings that each child had made while observing the successive changes in water levels and ask him to rearrange them in the correct order. Piaget found that the youngest children (around five or six) had difficulty in arranging the sheets in a series even though they had watched and recorded the successive water levels. As he has remarked frequently, "A sequence of perceptions does not in itself constitute a perception of a sequence."[12] These children had obviously not perceived the sequence of events, even though they had observed and drawn the water levels themselves. Older children had no difficulty in arranging the drawings in serial order.

As a final step in the experiment, Piaget cut each child's drawings in half so that I's and II's were all shuffled together, and then asked him to rearrange them correctly. Here the children from six to nine (mean age seven years, eight months) had great difficulty. Most of them could arrange both I and II in correct order separately, but could not correlate them. They might combine pairs of I and II by sheer guesswork, but could not remember or reconstruct a double series based on falling levels of I correlated with rising levels of II. Some children paired low levels of I and II, ignoring the inverse relationships which they had observed. Others paired the extremes correctly—that is, in inverse relationship—but went back to matching the other pairs directly. One boy, when questioned, explained, "The water rises and then it goes down again."[13] Piaget found this surprising, since children of eight and nine can arrange sticks or dolls in a series based on height, as we have seen. He finally concluded, after careful questioning, that the difficulty lay in the simultaneous coordination of two opposite motions—one rising, one falling.

Such an operation would be logically represented by the matrix form previously discussed (see Chapter 7). It involves the multiplication of a double series which, unlike the glasses in our previous illustration, has an inverse relationship; as one series increases, the other decreases. The children had an intuitive grasp of the over-all order of events but were unable to correlate them two at a time. To do this requires reversibility— the characteristic of operational thought which allows it to go backward in time and reconstruct past events. When only one series is involved, the time sequence is the same as the space series (water levels in this case). But when two different series must be matched in the same time, children have great difficulty in establishing simultaneity (coordination of events happening at the same time). Piaget found that it was not until between eight and nine years that his subjects could arrange events in series and then correlate that series with another. Through this temporal succession of events, they gradually developed the concept of time. This led Piaget to the conclusion that "the operations of seriation and co-seriation (serial correspondence) are prerequisites of the construction of time (order of co-placements) and not its consequence."[14]

But there is an aspect of time other than that of succession of events, and that is the aspect of duration, of length of time intervals. We have already referred to the youngsters who reported that the faster drawing or rapping or ticking of a metronome took more time than did slower motions. Using the same flask experiment, Piaget studied the development of the realization that velocity is inversely proportional to time—in other words, more rapid = less time. To show how the idea of time becomes divorced from speed or distance, he used the time intervals necessary for water to drop from I to II (expressed as $I_1 II_1$ for the first interval, $I_2 II_2$ for the second, etc.). Now these intervals were all equal, but because of the pear shape of the upper flask I, the water level fell slowly at first, and more rapidly in the narrow point. But in the lower glass II, the levels rose equally each time because of its cylindrical shape. Piaget marked these intervals (referred to as A, B, C, etc.) clearly on the two glasses and then asked his subjects whether the time required for the changes in water level were the same or different. He found in the youngest subjects that the greater perceptible displacement was considered to take more time (the water in I has "further to go" or "it drops down more quickly"). Again, as in the conservation experiments previously discussed, the children succumbed to the perceptual illusion of greater size or activity, and equated that with longer time.

Figure 21

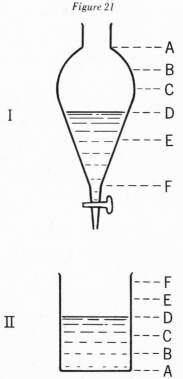

In the second stage, Piaget found that children began to grasp intuitively that time and speed are inversely proportional. This might have been due, he thought, to experiences such as racing with other children, in which two youngsters starting and stopping simultaneously do not end up at the same point because one child runs faster than the other. As a result of such observations, children learn to dissociate the amount of activity from the time interval involved, and realize that time is inversely proportional to speed. Another problem that had to be solved in this second stage, Piaget found, was the equality of the time intervals. The children did not realize that it took the same length of time for the water to drop from gradation I_1 to gradation I_2 in the upper flask, and to rise from II_1 to II_2 in the lower. Since the upper gradations changed with the shape of the flask, while the lower gradations were constant, the younger subjects had much difficulty. Some thought that the lower levels rose more quickly, some that "it drops down much more quickly," or "it takes less time to drop down than to rise." One boy argued that the length of time could be compared only in identical glasses; another that "it wasn't the same time because we didn't go at the same speed." Even when told that equal amounts of water were transferred at each interval, and that the rate of flow was constant, Stage II youngsters had trouble understanding that the time intervals in each case were the same. One nine-year-old, guided by Piaget's questions, finally realized, "Oh, it's the same thing . . . because it's the same number"—meaning the amount of water.

Children at the Stage III level of thinking, however, were able to deduce the equality of the time intervals, either because the amounts of water that ran out were the same or because the starting and finishing points were simultaneous. As one youngster put it, "The water drops and rises at the same time . . . while this one empties, the other one gets filled." The difference in the older children's approach to the problem is illustrated by the following:

Lad (8;7): "Did these two take the same time (I_1 I_2 and II_1 II_2)? *Yes, they did, because they're divided the same way.* Are they the same height? *No, this one* (I_1 I_2) *is smaller but that's because it's bigger* (wider). And what about these (I_1 I_3 and II_3 II_5)? *Oh yes, they took the same time because two equal amounts were poured out; it's the same parts of water.* And these (I_2 I_3 and I_6 I_7)? *Oh yes, they took the same time as well.* Why? *Because it's the same amount of water* (points to II_2 II_3 and II_6 II_7). And if we poured this lot (II_6 II_7) into here (I) ? *It would make a layer like that one* (I_6 I_7)."[15]

Here Lad is clearly not deceived by the different-sized intervals in I and II. His thinking shows the flexibility and reversibility characteristic of operational thought. He can go back in time and tell what would happen if the water in II_6 II_7 was poured back into I. Children of this age (eight or nine), says Piaget, are now ready to move on to the notion of isochronal time, which is measured in equal, recurring intervals. They have accomplished a sequence of logical operations, as follows:

1. The seriation of before and after, or the sequential ordering of events or $A \rightarrow B \rightarrow C$, $I_1 \rightarrow I_2 \rightarrow I_3$. Included in this seriation is the co-seriation of simultaneous events, as shown in the flask experiment.

$$I_1 \rightarrow I_2 \rightarrow I_3$$
$$\downarrow \quad \downarrow \quad \downarrow$$
$$II_1 \rightarrow II_2 \rightarrow II_3$$

2. The inclusive relationship of intervals which constitutes durations.

$$AB < AC < AD$$

3. The coordination of durations as intervals between events with the sequence of succession of such events.

$$A \rightarrow B \rightarrow C$$
$$AB \rightarrow BC$$
$$AC$$

4. Once these operations have been accomplished, the concept of measurement can be attained.

$$AB = BC = CD$$
$$AC = 2AB, AD = 3AB$$

The youngster who can logically infer the equality of synchronous durations of time is now ready to construct a time scale. If each unit of water were to equal five minutes of time, an hourglass could be constructed using the equipment in this experiment. Instead of this, however, Piaget used a large sandglass and a laboratory stopwatch. He assigned different activities to the children (i.e., walking around the table, putting marbles in a jar) and found that the youngest ones again equated time with speed. They declared that the sand fell faster when they were more active; therefore more work = more time. Even when they were told to watch the second hand on the stopwatch, which they could see moving at a consistent rate, the little ones declared that the hand moved more quickly than they themselves did. This egocentric thinking showed that the five-year-olds had not yet achieved the notion of constant measured speed; they thought the watch hand moved in time with their movements rather than at a consistent rate.

At around six, however, Piaget's subjects began intuitively to assume the constancy of the watch, but still hesitated about the sand.

Map (6;6): "Did the sand run as quickly or more quickly? *More quickly. . . . No, the same way. . . . No. . . .* As quickly or more quickly? *As quickly.* Why did you think more quickly? *It just slipped out, but it's because I myself was going more quickly.* And the clock? *Always the same way.* It goes for the same time no matter whether you go quickly or slowly? *The same time.*"[16]

Piaget says that it is not until around seven or eight years of age that a child can grasp the concept of successive intervals of time corresponding to equal distances traversed successively on the face of a clock. In other words, children cannot learn to tell time with any real understanding until about second grade. Certainly there is rote learning and the association of numbers on the clock with specific events or TV shows. But the hours that first-grade teachers spend stamping clock faces on papers for their pupils so they can color in the hands correctly might well be spent in more effective ways. I well remember the frustration of trying to teach a class of bright six-year-olds to tell time. They learned to read so quickly; why did they have so much difficulty with hours and minutes? It is a pity that Piaget's research on time was not translated sooner—a lot of it could have been saved!

Piaget described many more of these ingenious experiments in his book, all leading to the conclusion that the concept of time depends upon speed. Naïve time is just lived; little children deal with time only in the present. But as they learn to order events and to become aware of intervals of time between them, there develops an intuitive understanding of time based on succession of events and duration of intervals. As long as events take place within a given time, they can be ordered by their position in space. The drawings of water pouring from the upper glass into the lower could be arranged on a spatial basis rather than a temporal one. But in order to measure time itself, the length of the interval in which events occur, the time intervals must be related to speeds. So we come back to a fundamental condition. Time can be measured only by the motion of bodies covering equal distances in equal intervals; that is, at a constant rate of speed. Whether it be the swing of a clock pendulum or the earth's motion around the sun, time is dependent on speed. This is Piaget's answer to Einstein's question. Speed is fundamental to the understanding of time and precedes it in the development of children's thinking. Therefore, in the next section we will consider the development of the concept of speed.

17

movement and speed

The concept of speed as a relationship between distance traversed and time passed does not begin to appear in children until nine or ten years of age, according to Piaget. It is a relatively sophisticated notion which is not stabilized until the period of formal operations, at eleven or twelve. But very early in life there is a primitive intuition of speed which is based on passing or overtaking. The baby has experienced balls which roll past him or objects which change their position in space, and he has learned to anticipate events that follow each other in serial order. As we saw in the study of time, however, this practical kind of experience is far from being operational thought. The fact that the child has a sequence of perceptions does not mean that he perceives them as a sequence.

This fact Piaget demonstrated very neatly by his experiments

to show how the child develops a sense of the order of succession of positions in space. He rolled colored wooden balls
through a cardboard tunnel in the order A (red), B (brown),
C (yellow), and asked the children to predict in what order
the beads would reappear at the other end (position 2). Then
he rolled the balls back again so that they would emerge in
the order CBA, and asked the same question. He found that

Figure 22

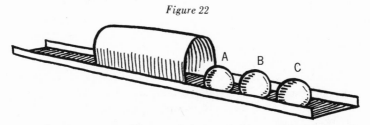

even the youngest subjects of four or five could predict the
ABC order. But when the balls rolled in the opposite direction
(position 1) they could not visualize the reverse order, CBA,
and were much surprised when C appeared first! There was
also confusion about the middle brown ball B. Young children
frequently predicted that the brown ball would emerge first, so
it could "have a turn." They did not understand that the relationship "between" would persist regardless of the direction of
movement.

Next Piaget varied the experiment. He rolled the balls into
the tunnel so they were hidden, and then asked the child to
sit on the opposite side of the table from where he had sat,
and make his prediction. He found that younger children confused their absolute position with relative position, and expected the balls to emerge in the opposite order from the way
they went in—as if the balls had reversed directions instead of
the child! In yet another variation Piaget would rotate the
whole tunnel one half-turn, or 180 degrees. This was done in
full view of the children, after the balls had already been rolled

into the tunnel in ABC order. Piaget then asked his subjects
to predict in what order the balls would emerge at position 2.
Since the ABC order which had been at position 1 was reversed
by the half-turn, the balls came out in CBA or inverse order.
When he turned the tunnel a full circle or 360 degrees, there
was of course no change and the balls came out in ABC or
direct order. But the younger children became hopelessly confused and muddled by these changes, as the following illustrates:

An (4 years) : "Which will come first out of the tunnel? *The
red one* (A). And then? *The brown one* (B) *and the yellow* (C).
[Demonstration.] And now they are coming back, which one will
come out first? *The red one, the brown, and the yellow one. Look!*
[Demonstration.] *Oh, no, it's the yellow, then the brown and the
red.* Why? *Because coming back it's the yellow one.* Fine. And
now, look, I'm turning the tunnel. . . . Which will be first this
time? *The red, then the brown, then the yellow one.* Look!
[Demonstration.] *It's the yellow one.* Why? *Because I didn't
know.* We'll start again. *It will be the yellow one.* [Demonstration.]
Why? *Don't know.*"[1]

Another experiment, using the same techniques, had three
little wooden dolls on a wire, passing back and forth behind
a screen. The first was blue, the second green, and the third
yellow. The results were much the same, with the Stage I
youngsters unable to predict the reverse order in which the
dolls would appear. The following example shows the firm con-
viction of a four-and-a-half-year-old that the middle figure
(green) would emerge first, despite Piaget's efforts to dissuade
her:

Ros (4;6) : "Which one will come out first? *Blue* (A) *then
green* (B) *then yellow* (C). And coming back? *Blue, green, yellow*
[going to demonstration]. *No, yellow, green, blue.* Look, now, I'm
turning it. . . . Which will be out first? *Blue.* [Demonstration.]
Right? *No.* Why not? *Because it's behind the yellow one. The bit*

of wire turned around. (New try). *Yellow.* [Demonstration.] *Yes.*
Why? *Because it turned the other way.* And after it? *Green.*
Why? *Because that's behind the yellow one.* (turning several
times) Which will be first? *Blue* (A) *or yellow* (C) *or green* (B).
Can the green one be first? *Yes.* How would it do that? . . .
(turning five or six times). Which do you think? *Green.* What's
that? . . . Look (showing the wire stem and the three dolls).
It can't. Why? *Because of the wire.* And now (turning more than
ten times)? *The green one this time!* Why? *It turned.* Was it at
the front? *In the middle.* And if you turn it, can that one come
first? *Yes.* Look! *No.* And this time (five more turns). Can the
green one be first? *Yes.*"[2]

Figure 23

A   B   C

These experiments show that preoperational children, from
four years on, have a primitive intuition of direct order, but
that they cannot reverse that order. They simply retrace, in
their minds, the events just as they were perceived, instead of
imagining an inversion. This is the rigidity of thought that
characterizes preoperational thinking, which we have already
seen in the toddler looking for his toy where he first saw it
hidden rather than where he last saw it. Even when a child
does recognize that he's wrong, he doesn't see why, as shown
by the inability to see that B will always be in the middle.

By the second stage, however, children close to or past six
can handle the inverse order of the dolls on the return journey

and are beginning to understand the invariability of the middle position:

Chri (5;4) : "Look at these beads going into the tunnel. How will they come out on the other side? *Red* (A) *first, then black* (B) *and blue* (C) *last.* Good. And now I'm making them come back. So? *Blue* (C) *first, then black* (B) *then red* (A). Why are they the other way? *Because you're coming from the other direction.* Fine. Now, look: I'm sending them in as I did before, as on your drawing, then I'm going to turn the tunnel over. Which is first? *Red* (A). Why? *Because the wire is the other way.* And then? *Black* (B) *and blue* (C). Look: they're going in now and I'm turn- ing the tunnel like that (half turn). Which will be first? *Red* (A). (Exp.). Is that right? *No. It's blue because you made it go the other way.* Let's start again (same explan.). Which first? *Red* (A) *because the wire is this side.* Look (exp.). *Oh, no, blue again be- cause it was turned the other way.* (Start again). And now? *Blue* (correct). And now, listen: I'm going to turn it twice, not just once any more. Which first? *Blue.* Why? *Because it was turned the other way.* Look. (exp.). *Oh, no, red! I thought it would come out on the other side.* (Several turns). Which would it be now? *Red or blue.* Why? *Or else black.* Why? *Oh, no, it couldn't because it's in the middle.*"[3]

There is still difficulty, however, with the effects of rotating the tunnel, even among seven-year-olds. Some can manage three or four half-turns and then become exhausted and make mistakes. Others can manage turns in succession but are lost when the experimenter jumps from one number to another, as in the following:

Pia (7 years) : "*Yellow* (C) *because before it was the blue one* (A). (Two turns or 360°)? *Blue or yellow.* Look. (One turn and one more turn slowly)? *Blue* (A) *because it starts off first and if you turn this once it's yellow* (C) *and if you turn it again it's blue* (A) *once more.* Four times? *Blue* (A) *because it's blue, yellow, blue, then yellow and blue again.* Five times? (He works it out again). *Yellow.* Six times? *Blue.* Three times? *Blue* (wrong). Eleven times? *Blue* (wrong). And black (B)? *No because that's*

*always in the middle: it can't get out because of the others be-
side it.*"[4]

It is not until Stage III that children are able to deal operationally with these changes in position. At this point they can
generalize that the ABC order occurs with even numbers of
180-degree rotations and CBA with odd numbers, even though
they may not know the categories "odd" and "even." One
little boy teased Piaget, telling him, "I can see through the
cardboard."[5]

Here we see the typical development of a child's thought
from the stage at which the experiment is observed but not
understood to the point of abstract generalization and reversibility of thought. Piaget used these experiments as examples of
the role of experience in the construction of mathematical
relationships. These are experiments the child is really making
on himself, on his own actions and sense of direction, rather
than on the objects to which his actions are applied. As in the
experiment with the colored balls, the child moves his relationship to the objects and then perceives the changes that take
place in them. Thus he constructs his notions of order, number, and space.

According to Piaget, the simplest intuition of speed as well
as of movement is based on this intuition of order. When a
body moving parallel to another body overtakes it, the child
notes that the overtaking body is moving faster, because it
has changed positions with the body which formerly preceded
it. In his characteristically thorough way, Piaget studied this
phenomenon in a three-part experiment. First he had two
tunnels, a long one and a short one, lined up evenly at one
end. He had little wooden men wired to go through the tunnels,
starting at the same time and emerging from the far ends of
the tunnels at the same moment. The child, who had already
pointed out which tunnel was longer, was now asked whether

one of the little men went faster than the other. The little children in Stage I would say that they went at the same speed because they emerged at the same time. Piaget would say, "Isn't one tunnel longer than the other?" and they would say that it was. "Well, then," Piaget would say, "did they go at the same speed?" And the children would say, "Yes, because they came out together."

Next Piaget removed the tunnels, so the little men were visible to his young subjects. When they could see one overtaking the other, the children agreed that the second one moved faster than the first. Last, Piaget replaced the tunnels and repeated the original experiment. Once again, the young children would return to their original statements: the two men moved at the same speed.

Ios (5;6) : "Did they set off at the same time? *Yes.* And stopped at the same time? *Yes.* Did one of the dolls go faster than the other? *No.* Are the tunnels the same length? *No, this one is smaller and this one bigger.* Then was one of the dolls faster? *No.* Watch again (repeat experiment). *Yes, the same speed.* In the smaller tunnel is the road shorter? *Yes.* And they arrive at the same time? *Yes.* Then does one go quicker than the other? *No.* Does it make no difference if one of the tunnels is bigger than the other? *Of course not!* Which is the longer road? *This one.* Then does one of them go faster than the other if they arrive at the same time? *No.*"

(The two paths travelled under the tunnels are marked with chalk and the tunnels removed.) "If they start at the same time and stop at the same time, does one go quicker than the other? *Yes— the first one goes quicker because the path is longer.* (We rub out the chalk and replace the tunnels.) Do they start and finish together? *Yes.* Does one go faster than the other? *No.* Why? *They stop at the same time.*"[6]

Here the child's statement, "the first one goes faster because the road is longer," sounds like an intuitive grasp of speed based on a relationship between time spent and distance traversed. However, the fact that he returns to his original error when the men are no longer visible indicates that his intuition is of a practical rather than an intellectual relationship. He sees the overtaking simply as an inversion of order; this is the primitive early intuition of speed.

In order to separate the notions of farther or nearer (the order of points of arrival) from the notion of length (the interval between the starting and stopping points) Piaget devised the following experiment with very interesting results. Using string stretched around tacks hammered into a piece of board, he created two "roads," one straight and the other angled as shown in Figure 24. On each string was a bead representing a

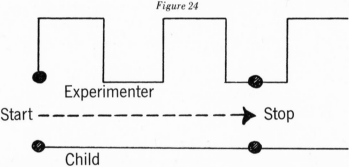

Figure 24

streetcar which could slide along the roads. Piaget moved his bead along the angled road and the child moved his along the straight road. Piaget's directions were: "I'm going to travel along this road, and then you are going to travel along your road exactly the same distance I did. You are to go over just as much road as I do." Piaget would then move his bead two segments as shown in Figure 24, and the Stage I child would move his opposite Piaget's. When Piaget pointed out that he had gone "all the way," one five-and-a-half-year-old said to him, "It's the same distance because this one [A_2] is here [i.e., above] and that one [A_1] is there" (right underneath).[7] Piaget then started over, moved his bead to the next segment, and stopped midway on a right-angle line as in Figure 25. Again the child would stop parallel to Piaget's position. Finally,

Figure 25

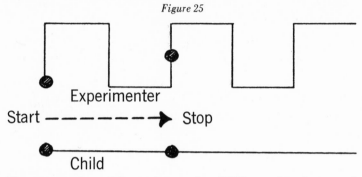

Piaget moved at right angles to the child's road and stopped as shown in Figure 26. This would confuse the youngster, who would say, "But I'm there," or move just a fraction. When

Figure 26

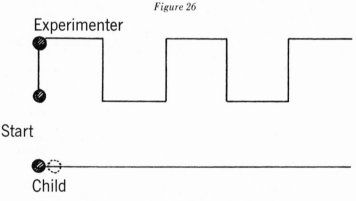

Piaget pointed out that he had moved much farther, or asked, "Have they gone the same distance?" the child would answer, "Yes, because they're opposite."

In other words, to the children under six, going the same distance meant simply not passing each other. Distance was defined in terms of overtaking rather than of intervals of length. So Piaget tried providing a cardboard ruler, which the children in Stage II began to use, but inaccurately, most preferring to gauge the distance visually. Gradually, however, the older subjects showed improvement, until between seven and eight they were able to make a comparison of the distances traversed and measure them accurately.

Having studied the effect of order of positions and distances traversed, Piaget turned to a study of relative movements. He used pairs of toy cars moving parallel to each other, but with one car moving up from behind and overtaking the second. The distance between the two cars thus grew smaller and smaller until they were even, and then grew larger and larger. Yet if the two cars stopped at the same time, the Stage I children would say that they traveled at equal speeds. As Piaget remarked, "It is as if the child judged speed by the finishing point alone, regardless of the distance travelled."[8] This experiment indicates once more that the primitive intuition of speed is relative only to the order of positions, not to time spent or distance traveled. Piaget found that if he increased the relative speeds of the cars from the normal ratio of 2 to 1 to a very obvious difference of 4 or 6 to 1, the Stage I child would briefly acknowledge that one car went faster. But a moment later he would slip back into his original error, because it fitted his intuitive logic.

Eri (5;0) (Blue catches up on red): "Was one going harder? *Both the same.* How do you know? *Because one went as fast as the other.* Did one go a longer distance? *Yes, the blue one.* Then was one going harder than the other? *No.*"

(Red overtakes blue): "Was one going harder? *One of them was farther ahead, the red one.* Was that one going harder? *A bit more. It was not going fast, but it was farther ahead.* And the blue one? *Not so hard: it was away behind.*"

(Red almost catches up with blue, travelling almost twice as far in the same time): "*The blue one was farther ahead, the red one was away behind.* We were all of them going harder? *Blue.* Where did it start from? *From here.* Did one do a longer distance? *No, yes, red.* Can you tell if one was faster, going harder? *The red one was slower and the blue one faster.* Why? *Because I can see that it is ahead of the other one.* Which has the longer distance? *The red one.* Which one was faster? *The blue one.* Why? *Because it is ahead of the other one.*"[9]

Here the child's thinking is similar to that observed in the conservation experiments with clay. The child's attention is centered on the stopping points as if they were absolutes; he is unable also to take into account the starting point, or total distances covered. When he is forced, by the dramatic increase of the speed of one car, to turn his attention to the distance covered, he goes through a period of disequilibrium, just like the child who alternately centers on the length, and then the width, of the clay. Finally at around nine or ten he is able to carry both positions—starting as well as stopping—in his mind. If the cars start and stop at the same time, and one covers a greater distance, he can then conclude that it has traveled faster. These experiments make it clear why children cannot handle problems of the Rate × Time = Distance type, until they are at least in the fourth grade. For slow learners, using toy cars as Piaget did in these experiments would make the relationships much clearer than reading about them in an arithmetic workbook.

Piaget described many more experiments, using bodies with unequal speeds and going in different directions, or bodies which accelerate in speed, to show how children achieve the concept of speed based on a ratio between distance and time. In the concluding chapter of *The Child's Conception of Movement and Speed*, he methodically sums up six different kinds of operations used, beginning with operations of placement and displacement, and culminating in metrical operations. These, through the use of repeatable units, permit measurements of distances and time intervals, leading to the concept of speed $(S = D/T)$.

It is interesting to note that the concepts of both time and speed follow parallel courses in their development. Both are based on a primitive concept of order: order of events in time and order of positions in speed. Piaget points out that in judging speed on the basis of overtaking, or passing, the child has escaped from the chicken-and-egg problem which has plagued the physicists; time measured by speed, and speed defined by time. To the child, time is a coordination of speeds; but speed is independent of time and depends on the order of passing positions in space. When he can take account not only of the order of passing but of the distance covered, the child is ready for the operational concept of speed as a relationship between space (distance) and time.

18

education

Education today is in a state of tremendous crisis. Teachers go on strike, students stage rebellions, parents attack the school boards and vote down their budgets. Principals and teachers are resigning right and left, and even the Commissioner of Education for the United States was fired by the President in 1970.

In the midst of all this uproar the cool, reasonable voice of Piaget can be heard, pointing out a few hard facts and clarifying the issues now clouded in emotion. *Science of Education and the Psychology of the Child*, published in 1970, is a translation of two papers, one written in 1935 and the other in 1965. In them he offers the wisdom garnered from many years of observing children and participating in academic life. There is no mincing of words here; Piaget feels that many teachers are using archaic educational methods and that their students who are not actively alienated are sitting passively in classes which they find meaningless and irrelevant. Learning, far from being interesting and challenging, becomes a string of boring facts, completely divorced from thought and feeling. Is it any wonder that our youngsters are dropping out and turning on?

Piaget points out that even after all these years we have not clearly answered some of the most fundamental questions about education.

1. *What is the aim of teaching?* Is it to accumulate useful knowledge? If so, "useful" in what sense? How much does the little girl who wants to become a manicurist need to know about the French and Indian Wars? Do we want our students exposed to certain required areas of the curriculum? Is our aim to have them pass tests on subject matter? To teach them to think creatively and innovatively? To know how to check, verify, and criticize new information? Or to rattle off a string of facts in the order required by the teacher? Is it the aims of the teacher or the aims of the student, or both, that we should be considering?

2. *What should we teach?* What areas of knowledge should be part of the curriculum, and at what level? What areas are necessary and what irrelevant? Should we throw out the classics to make room for Black Studies? Should we teach handwriting in the elementary school? Is sex education the school's responsibility or the parents'?

3. *How should we teach?* Are talking typewriters and programmed learning machines more effective than teachers? Should we have structured classrooms, or "individualized learning"? Should we teach reading by the phonetic or the "whole word" approach?

These are only three of the questions still unanswered in education today. And according to Piaget, they never will be answered until educators turn to experimental research for decisive information. To him, it is shocking and "scarcely believable that in a field so accessible to experiment . . . the pedagogue has not organized sustained and methodical experiments, but has remained content to decide . . . on the basis of opinions whose 'common sense' in fact conceals more affectivity (emotion) than effective reasoning."[1] About the only way we have of judging the effectiveness of our educational methods is to rely on school grades and certain competitive examinations such as College Boards. To do this leads us into a vicious circle because much of the work done in school is directed toward passing those examinations; how, then, can they be considered a fair criterion of the effectiveness of education? What *should* be done, says Piaget, is to test after several years and see how much of that learning is retained when the examinations are forgotten. Or better yet, "compare the results of schools without examinations, where the students' worth is evaluated by the teachers as a function of work done throughout the year, with those ordinary schools where the prospect of final examinations may be falsifying not only the work of students, but even that of teachers as well."[2]

The fact that on such fundamental questions educational research "still remains silent" is to Piaget mute testimony to "the terrifying disproportion that still subsists between the scope or importance of the problems facing it, and the means being employed to resolve them."[3] With more and more children pouring into the schools, their futures dependent on the answers to these and other questions, Piaget sees only the most meager basic research taking place in education, and the prospect appalls him.

Why should this be so? asks Piaget. Why, in an age when sociology, psychology, anthropology, and other social sciences all have a broad basis of scientific knowledge, is education so far behind? The answer rings out clear and honest: education is not considered a science, but rather a second-rate profession. The schoolteacher is lacking in social status and intellectual prestige. It is difficult to get good people into education because of relatively low salaries. The teacher is not thought of, by himself or anyone else, as a specialist in techniques and scientific creativity, "but rather as the mere transmitter of a kind of knowledge that is within everyone's grasp. In other words, it is considered that a good teacher is providing what is expected of him when he is in possession of a general elementary education and has learned a few appropriate formulas that enable him to inculcate similar education in the minds of his pupils."[4]

It is clear that the public (which includes "certain educational authorities" and most of the teachers themselves) does not recognize teaching as a difficult and complex science. Instead of working, as does a doctor, under the jurisdiction of professional associations made up of other doctors, teachers are forced to conform to programs and methods dictated by the school administration or state departments of education. These bodies are generally made up of gentlemen who, if they ever taught inside a classroom, escaped as soon as possible. The teachers therefore, are extremely restricted, as compared to other professionals, by a bureaucracy which has little time to devote to the research which is education's crying need. Moreover, at professional meetings of educators, as compared with medical or psychological conventions, Piaget says, "one cannot but be struck by the prevailing lack of scientific dynamism . . . when discussing [educational] problems."[5] The author, who has attended many educational conferences, has often dozed off, because of this "lack of scientific dynamism."

The last criticism Piaget levels at the teaching profession is also the most serious; it is directed at the teacher-training institutes, which are often isolated from other university facilities and "entirely lack any direct link with . . . research." Although the situation in the United States is somewhat different from what Piaget describes in Europe, it is still true that the traditional system for training teachers has had a "deadly effect" upon educational research. "Cut off from the scientific trends and the atmosphere of research and experiment that could have injected new life into them,"[6] teachers here plug along through their required credits in education and go through the motions of performing a single piece of research, which they hand in with a sigh of relief, never to undertake any more. Though Piaget has kind words for American "departments of education" as being less isolated than European training institutes, he notes accurately that child psychology is often taught in the education department. This means that the experimental psychology department does its research on rats, "which has often had a somewhat disastrous effect."[7] Another disadvantage which he candidly mentions is the possibility that "mathematicians, physicists, and biologists who have not succeeded in their own fields . . . find outlets in the Departments of Education for teaching the didactics of mathematics, physics, biology, and so on—a state of affairs that is not always of great advantage to the progress of pedagogical research."[8] While no one would deny that there are great and creative professors in departments of education, there are many more mediocre ones who get bogged down in the nitty-gritty of methods and lesson plans.

The fundamental problem, according to Piaget, is that educators are more interested in teaching than they are in children. Their concentration, their training, is upon methods and curriculum. Their knowledge of child psychology is often sketchy; their interest in the child's mental and emotional development limited. Teachers want to teach and have children listen; but

this, we have seen, is the antithesis of how children learn! Over
and over, through these pages, we have heard Piaget saying,
"Knowledge is derived from action. . . . To know an object
is to act upon it and to transform it. . . . To know is therefore to assimilate reality into structures of transformation, and
these are the structures that intelligence constructs as a direct
extension of our actions."[9] From the baby who creeps after his
hidden toy, thereby constructing the notions of space and object
constancy, to the child who counts and seriates and measures,
constructing the notions of number, order, and weight, all
knowledge derives from the actions which the child performs
on the objects and then organizes in his brain. Children do not
learn by sitting passively in their seats, listening to the teacher,
any more than they learn to swim by sitting in rows on a wharf
watching grown-up swimmers in the water. "If the aim of intellectual training is to form the intelligence rather than to
stock the memory, and to produce intellectual explorers rather
than mere erudition, then traditional education is manifestly
guilty of a grave deficiency."[10]

Even the newer methods of lectures accompanied by demon-
strations are not as effective, says Piaget, as having the child
discover or invent ways of dealing with objects for himself. It
can be shown that even the accuracy of the memory of a tower
of cubes will differ among children depending on whether they
(a) simply looked at and perceived the cubes, (b) observed
the tower being constructed by an adult while the children
watched, or (c) reconstructed the tower themselves. The memories which result from the last treatment are clearly superior,
whereas there is not much difference between the other two.
This shows, says Piaget, "that by carrying out experiments in
the child's presence instead of making the child carry them out,
one loses the entire informational and formative value offered
by action proper as such."[11]

It is in this kind of basic research that education is woefully lacking, says Piaget. If student teachers were systematically required to observe and question children, they would learn much more about how children's minds develop and how they can be stimulated to think for themselves. But alas, the student teachers often suffer from the same kind of passive learning as their pupils; they may attend a set of lectures on child psychology and pass an examination without ever having really faced a child. Piaget feels that studying child psychology is not enough—teachers need to actually carry out their own research "to see how difficult it is to make themselves understood by the children, and to understand what the children are saying."[12] Teachers have the illusion, when they stand in front of classes, that they are understanding their students and are making themselves understood. Only performing actual research will make them realize how far they are from the truth. Children are often able to verbalize glibly without having any real comprehension of what they are talking about. This is why the intelligence of the middle-class child is sometimes overestimated by teachers, while that of the inarticulate ghetto child is frequently underestimated.

Piaget feels that all teachers should be active in research instead of just reading about it. He describes the primary school training program in Geneva, which requires that all student teachers take part in a year-long research program. Every afternoon is spent in the schools, working in groups of two or three under the supervision of a trained research assistant. The teachers learn how to question the children, how to record the facts, and how to evaluate the success or failure of their experiments. This, says Piaget, is an intellectual training which forces them to understand the complexity of the problems involved, far more than any professor's lecture. "It is by and through research that the teacher's profession ceases to be merely a trade and . . . acquires the dignity of all professions that draw upon both the arts and the sciences."[13]

Piaget is adamant in his insistence that not just primary but all teachers need this kind of training. Secondary school training emphasizes subject matter and methods but often neglects the psychology of the children being taught. The more enthusiastic a teacher is about his specialty, Piaget observes, the less interested he is likely to be in his students. "It often happens that future science teachers display an undisguised contempt for the psychology of development until one can succeed in making them grasp the epistemological bearing of the laws of that development."[14] In others words, science teachers may need to be persuaded that there is an "embryology· of intelligence" that develops according to natural laws, just as in other sciences. Once the formative processes involved in the acquisition of knowledge have been understood, they can be related to the teacher's special areas of interest to help him teach more effectively. Thus a mathematician is interested in how children develop the notions of number or geometry; a chemistry teacher can learn much from observing how youngsters handle the problem of combining chemical elements in Inhelder's and Piaget's experiment with the four flasks. This understanding of the mental processes of their students is just as important for them, Piaget believes, as it is for a nursery school teacher to understand the symbolic meaning of play, or an elementary school teacher to understand the morality of cooperation she sees emerging in her class.

Turning now from teacher training to the state of the schools, Piaget is all in favor of the "new methods of education" as opposed to the traditional approach. He refers frequently to "the active school" as opposed to one in which children experience "cognitive passivity." Through his activities at UNESCO, Piaget has had international influence on public education. His theories are reflected in the British "infant schools," in the "discovery method," "individualized learning," "personalized education," the "inductive method," "perceptual-motor training," and a host of other approaches. Basically, what he means by the "active method" is that children should be free to explore, question, and discover for themselves, either on the sensory-motor basis for young children or on the basis of internalized action or thought at the operational level. Children need to talk to one another, for that is how they learn. The teacher is not there to lecture and demonstrate, but to observe and question, as we have seen Piaget do in his experiments, in order to make children think and discover new solutions, new structures of thought. At a meeting of the International Bureau of Education in Geneva, Piaget once heard a Canadian say that in his province they had just decided every class should have two classrooms—one where the teacher is, and one where the teacher isn't. Piaget quoted this as the best idea he had ever heard from a teacher! He feels strongly that children need to take a more active part in their own education, because what they most need to learn is not facts, but an independent way of functioning. Much of what we teach children today will be outmoded by the time they graduate, but critical insight and creative ideas will always be needed. Piaget once said:

The principal goal of education is to create men who are capable of doing new things, not simply of repeating what other generations have done—men who are creative, inventive, and discoverers. The second goal of education is to form minds which can be critical, can verify, and not accept everything they are offered. The great danger today is of slogans, collective opinions, ready-made trends of thought. We have to be able to resist them individually, to criticize, to distinguish between what is proven and what is not. So we need pupils who are active, who learn early to find out by themselves, partly by their own spontaneous activity and partly through material we set up for them; who learn early to tell what is verifiable and what is simply the first idea to come to them.[15]

As an example of an "active school" let us describe one of the British infant schools (five to seven years), where Piaget's theories have helped to bring about a sweeping revolution. According to Rosemary Williams, who was head teacher at the Westfield Infants School in Leicestershire, teachers are given a great deal of freedom "so that they can teach as individuals and so the children can feel they are learning as individuals."[16] She described classrooms full of children busily reading, writing, painting, building, tending to pets. The hallways are used for science exhibits, art displays, workbenches, block constructions, and playing store. The children come in and take up whatever they want to do. Some will read quietly or listen to another child in the library alcove. Some will go to the dress-up corner or to the activity tables. Here all kinds of materials await them—on the number tables it might be buttons to count, beads to string, sugar or flour to measure, number lines, rulers, and commercial materials such as Stern blocks or Cuisenaire rods. The children are free to move about and talk with one another. The teacher circulates, listening, asking questions, helping with spelling or reading, advising. Her role is much less structured but much more sensitive and creative than that of the traditional schoolmistress. She must know when to let a child daydream and when to prod him on to something harder. She does not complain about children making a mess, for each child must clean up after himself. There is a great deal of "busy noise" in such a school, but children are not allowed to bother one another. In such an environment children learn quickly, because they *want* to learn. Their activities are their own choice, and they are not forced to sit still at one desk, listening in stultifying boredom while the teacher does all the talking![17]

It is only in this kind of setting, where a child's innate

curiosity and desire to learn is tapped, that true education takes place, according to Piaget. "The essential functions of intelligence consist in understanding and in inventing; in other words, building up structures by structuring reality."[18] A child, through his own "personal research," organizes objects into series, or classes, or numbers, and thus builds up the logical groupings of classes and relations which we have already discussed. Because he is interested in his own experiments does not mean that they do not involve effort; on the contrary, he is willing to work harder on a project that is his own, as anyone who has watched children is aware. This kind of teaching involves more effort on the part of the teacher, too; ". . . the active methods are much more difficult to employ than our current receptive methods," admits Piaget.[19] The teacher must be able to keep track of many more activities than if she stood at the front of the room, teaching one lesson to all. She must be more creative, more experienced, and better trained, with a thorough knowledge of children's emotional and intellectual development. "The heartbreaking difficulty of pedagogy, as indeed in medicine and in many other branches of knowledge that partake at the same time of art and science, is in the fact that the best methods are also the most difficult ones."[20]

Piaget takes a dim view of some of the modern aids to teaching. He feels that many educators with insufficient psychological background tend to confuse "active methods" with "intuitive methods." (We have pointed out that intuitive thinking is based on perception and is subject to error.) Thus the use of audio-visual materials such as films and television is seen as producing "figurative processes" rather than true operational processes. By this Piaget means that they produce perceptions or mental images which are merely a precise copy of what has been seen, rather than a really flexible, reversible, stable understanding. This is the same kind of rote learning approach that Piaget criticizes in programmed learning machines. Skinner's "teaching machines," he says, are a great success, if by success is meant merely the verbal reproduction of the desired answer.

The sentimental and the natural worriers have been saddened by the fact that schoolmasters can be replaced by machines. In my view . . . these machines have performed at least one great service for us, which is to demonstrate beyond all possible doubt the mechanical character of the schoolmaster's function as it is conceived by traditional teaching methods: if the ideal of that method is merely to elicit correct repetition of what has been correctly transmitted, then it goes without saying that a machine can fulfill those conditions correctly.[21]

In discussing needed reforms in education, Piaget comes out strongly for the abolition of examinations. He considers them harmful because "they polarize around the pursuit of ephemeral and largely artificial results the majority of the activities that ought to be concentrated upon the formation of the intelligence and good working methods."[22] He feels that examination marks are "variable, relatively arbitrary, and lacking in concrete significance." Good marks on examinations depend on memory and a kind of memory that has little place in real life; in fact it is a "mental artifact." One wonders whether Piaget would be in favor of the pass-fail grades which many students are now demanding. Clearly he feels that current methods of "cramming" are a waste of time. "The only genuine examination," he says, ". . . would be one in which the candidate is free to use his books, notes, etc., and accomplishes a certain amount of work that is merely a continuation of what he has been doing in class."[23]

In his dignified and erudite fashion Piaget is voicing the same criticisms of the schools that have been raised by John Holt, Jonathan Kozol, Jerome Bruner, George Dennison,

Charles Silberman, and a score of others in this country—not to mention the hordes of young people, from city slums to university campuses, who are rebelling against the "education-ist establishment." Two New York college professors have recently charged that the schools are strenuously engaged in stifling the intelligence and creativity of students while the "knowledge explosion" urgently demands that they most need to use their minds and talents effectively.[24] At a time when the whole world is crying out for new ways of educating children to meet the demands of rising populations and dwindling teaching staffs, Piaget here points out some much-needed changes. Our school systems, he says, were constructed by conservatives who were more interested in traditional practices than in training inventive and critical minds. "From the point of view of society's present needs, it is apparent that those old molds are cracking in order to make way for broader, more flexible systems and more active methods."[25] But the teachers, who have not been given "any opportunity for initiative and even less for research and discovery," are thereby imprisoned in their present lowly status.

And now, at the moment when we are witnessing an educational revolution of great historical importance, since it is centered on the child and the adolescent, and on precisely those qualities they possess that will be most useful to tomorrow's society, the teachers in our various schools can command neither a science of education sufficiently advanced to permit personal efforts on their part that would contribute to the future progress of that discipline, nor the solid consideration that would be attached to such a scientific, practical, and socially essential form of activity: as a consequence, the teacher's position exerts no attraction and the recruitment of teachers becomes increasingly difficult.[26]

The problem of teacher training is, then, the key problem upon whose solution the fate of the schools depends. Piaget has shown us how this problem must be solved—by giving teachers more initiative, more freedom, and a better foundation in child psychology and research. Anyone who has tried to do research in the public schools today knows how difficult it is to get permission to work with a group of children. Proposals get bogged down in bureaucratic red tape, and principals are afraid to ask for parental consent. The schools have been paying lip service to "learning by doing" since the days of Dewey —but most of the time it is merely a cliché. Piaget has shown us, in his thorough and painstaking studies of the child, that verbal understanding is superficial and "deforming"; learning, whether for children or their teachers, comes only through the subject's own activity. The ability and eagerness to learn, which is part of every child's birthright, is our greatest educational resource. If we can learn to develop this great human potential, instead of stifling it, we can solve the problems of despair in the slums and rebellion on the campuses which plague our country today. This is Piaget's message.

Outline of Piaget's Periods of Cognitive Development

SENSORY-MOTOR PERIOD (FIRST TWO YEARS)

Stage I (0–1 month)—Characterized by neonatal reflexes and gross, uncoordinated body movements. Stage of complete egocentrism with no distinction between self and outer reality; no awareness of self as such.

Stage II (1–4 months)—New response patterns are formed by chance from combinations of primitive reflexes. The baby's fist accidentally finds its way into his mouth through a coordination of arm moving and sucking.

Stage III (4–8 months)—New response patterns are coordinated and repeated intentionally in order to maintain interesting changes in the environment.

Stage IV (8–12 months)—More complex coordinations of previous behavior patterns, both motor and perceptual. Baby pushes aside obstacles or uses parent's hand as a means to a desired end. Emergence of anticipatory and intentional behavior; beginning of search for vanished objects.

Stage V (12–18 months)—Familiar behavior patterns varied in different ways as if to observe different results. Emergence of directed groping toward a goal, and of new means-end manipulations for reaching desired objects.

Stage VI (1½–2 years)—Internalization of sensory-motor behavior patterns and beginnings of symbolic representation. Invention of new means through internal experimentation rather than external trial and error.

PREOPERATIONAL PERIOD (TWO TO SEVEN YEARS)

Characterized by egocentric thinking expressed in animism, artificialism, realism, and magic omnipotence.

Preconceptual Stage (2–4 years)—Development of perceptual constancy and of representation through drawings, language, dreams, and symbolic play. Beginnings of first overgeneralized attempts at conceptualization, in which representatives of a class are not distinguished from the class itself (e.g., all dogs are called by the name of the child's own dog).

Perceptual or Intuitive Stage (4–7 years)—Prelogical reasoning appears, based on perceptual appearances untempered by reversibility (e.g., Grandma in a new hat is no longer recognized as Grandma). Trial and error may lead to an intuitive discovery of correct relationships, but the child is unable to take more than one attribute into account at one time (e.g., brown beads cannot at the same time be wooden beads).

CONCRETE OPERATIONAL PERIOD (SEVEN TO ELEVEN YEARS)

Characterized by thought that is logical and reversible. The child understands the logic of classes and relations and can coordinate series and part-whole relationships dealing with concrete things.

FORMAL OPERATIONAL PERIOD (ELEVEN YEARS TO ADULTHOOD)

Characterized by the logic of propositions, the ability to reason from a hypothesis to all its conclusions, however theoretical. This involves second-order operations, or thinking about thoughts or theories rather than concrete realities.

Piaget's Works in Chronological Order According to French Publication Dates
(INCLUDING EARLIEST ENGLISH PUBLICATIONS)

I. Studies of the Language, Logic, and Morality of the Pre-operational Child

1924 *The Language and Thought of the Child.* New York: Harcourt, Brace & World, 1926.

1924 *Judgment and Reasoning in the Child.* New York: Harcourt, Brace & World, 1928.

1926 *The Child's Conception of the World.* New York: Harcourt, Brace & World, 1929; London: Routledge & Kegan Paul, 1929.

1927 *The Child's Conception of Physical Causality.* London: Routledge & Kegan Paul, 1930.

1932 *The Moral Judgment of the Child.* New York: Macmillan, 1955; London: Routledge & Kegan Paul, 1932.

II. Studies of the Beginnings of Intelligence, Based on Piaget's Observations of His Own Babies During the Sensory-Motor Period

1936 *The Origins of Intelligence in Children.* New York: International Universities Press, 1952.

1937   *The Construction of Reality in the Child.* New York: Basic Books, 1954.

1945   *Play, Dreams and Imitation in Childhood.* New York: Norton, 1951; London: Heinemann, 1951.

III. Logico-Mathematical Formulations of the Development of Operational Thinking

1941   *The Child's Conception of Number.* New York: Humanities Press, 1952.

1946   *The Child's Conception of Time.* New York: Basic Books, 1970; London: Routledge & Kegan Paul, 1969.

1946   *The Child's Conception of Movement and Speed.* New York: Basic Books, 1970; London: Routledge & Kegan Paul, 1970.

1947   *The Psychology of Intelligence.* New York: Harcourt Brace, 1950; London: Routledge & Kegan Paul, 1950.

1948   With Bärbel Inhelder. *The Child's Conception of Space.* New York: Humanities Press, 1956; London: Routledge & Kegan Paul, 1956.

1953   *Logic and Psychology.* New York: Basic Books, 1957; London: Routledge & Kegan Paul, 1953. (Out of print.)

1956   With Bärbel Inhelder. *The Growth of Logical Thinking from Childhood to Adolescence.* New York: Basic Books, 1958.

1959   With Bärbel Inhelder. *The Early Growth of Logic in the Child.* New York: Harper & Row, 1964; London: Routledge & Kegan Paul, 1964.

1960   With Bärbel Inhelder and Alina Szeminska. *The Child's Conception of Geometry.* New York: Basic Books, 1960; London: Routledge & Kegan Paul, 1960.

1961   *The Mechanisms of Perception.* New York: Basic Books, 1969; London: Routledge & Kegan Paul, 1969.

1964   *Six Psychological Studies.* New York: Random House, 1967.

1966   With Bärbel Inhelder. *The Psychology of the Child.* New York: Basic Books, 1969.

1966   With Bärbel Inhelder et al. *Mental Imagery in the Child.* New York: Basic Books, 1971.

1968   *Genetic Epistemology.* New York: Columbia University

Press, 1970. (The Woodbridge Lectures, given at Columbia University, in 1968; not published in French.)

1968 *Structuralism*. New York: Basic Books, 1970.

1969 *Science of Education and the Psychology of the Child*. New York: Orion Press, 1970.

notes

Chapter 1   Piaget: A Profile

1. Piaget, "Autobiography," in E. G. Boring, et al., *History of Psychology in Autobiography*, Vol. 4, p. 237.
2. *Ibid.*, p. 238.
3. *Ibid.*, p. 240.
4. David Elkind, "Giant in the Nursery—Jean Piaget," *The New York Times Magazine*, May 26, 1968, pp. 25 ff. Republished in *Children and Adolescents: Interpretive Essays on Jean Piaget*, p. 9.

Chapter 2   Adaptation: The Basis of Behavior

1. Piaget, *Six Psychological Studies*, p. 3.
2. See, for example, Elkind, *Children and Adolescents*, p. 108; Jerome Bruner, *The Process of Education*; and Monique Laurendeau and Adrien Pinard, *Causal Thinking in the Child: A Genetic and Experimental Approach*.

Chapter 3 The Beginnings of Intelligence

1. Piaget, *The Origins of Intelligence in Children*, p. 110.
2. Piaget, *Six Psychological Studies*, p. 4.
3. See *Six Psychological Studies;* and "Development and Learning" in Richard E. Ripple and Verne O. Rockcastle (eds.), *Piaget Rediscovered*.
4. Piaget, *Six Psychological Studies*, p. 9.
5. *Ibid.*, p. 10.
6. Piaget, *The Origins of Intelligence in Children*, p. 159.
7. *Ibid.*, p. 217.
8. *Ibid.*, p. 291.

Chapter 5 Conservation

1. Reported in a series of articles in *Scandinavian Journal of Psychology* (1961), some of which have been reprinted in Irving E. Sigel and Frank H. Hooper (eds.), *Logical Thinking in Children*, pp. 265–295.
2. Ripple and Rockcastle, *Piaget Rediscovered*, p. 11.
3. Piaget, *The Origins of Intelligence in Children*, p. 30.
4. Elkind, *Children and Adolescents*, p. 18.
5. Piaget, Bärbel Inhelder, and Alina Szeminska, *The Child's Conception of Geometry*, pp. 95–101.
6. Ripple and Rockcastle, *Piaget Rediscovered*, p. 17.

Chapter 6 The Preoperational Child

1. Piaget, *The Language and Thought of the Child.*
2. Piaget, *The Moral Judgment of the Child*, p. 24.
3. Piaget, *The Child's Conception of the World*, p. 9.
4. Wayne Dennis, "Piaget's Questions Applied to a Child of Known Environment," *Journal of Genetic Psychology*, 60 (1942), 307–320.
5. Piaget, *Play, Dreams, and Imitation in Childhood*, p. 258.
6. Elkind, *Children and Adolescents*, p. 12.
7. Piaget, *The Child's Conception of the World*, p. 220.
8. Roger W. Russell and Wayne Dennis, "Studies in Animism: I. A Standardized Procedure for the Investigation of Animism," *Journal of Genetic Psychology*, 55 (1939), 389–400.

9. Piaget, *The Child's Conception of the World*, p. 64.

10. *Ibid.*, p. 94.

11. *Ibid.*, pp. 110–111.

12. Piaget, *Play, Dreams, and Imitation in Childhood*, p. 224.

13. *Ibid.*, p. 225

Chapter 7   Concrete Operations

1. John H. Flavell, *The Developmental Psychology of Jean Piaget*.

2. Alfred L. Baldwin, *Theories of Child Development*.

3. Bärbel Inhelder and Jean Piaget, *The Growth of Logical Thinking from Childhood to Adolescence;* and also *The Early Growth of Logic in the Child*.

4. Flavell, *Developmental Psychology of Jean Piaget*, p. 187.

5. Inhelder and Piaget, *The Early Growth of Logic in the Child*, p. 22.

6. *Ibid.*, p. 55.

7. Piaget, *The Child's Conception of Number*, p. 164.

8. *Ibid.*, p. 176.

9. Bruner, et al., *Studies in Cognitive Growth*, pp. 154 ff.

10. Flavell, *Developmental Psychology of Jean Piaget*, p. 192.

Chapter 8   Formal Operations

1. Inhelder and Piaget, *The Growth of Logical Thinking from Childhood to Adolescence*, p. xxiii.

2. *Ibid.*, pp. 174–175.

3. Flavell, *Developmental Psychology of Jean Piaget*.

4. Baldwin, *Theories of Child Development*.

5. Inhelder and Piaget, *Growth of Logical Thinking*, p. 111.

6. *Ibid.*, pp. 114–115.

7. *Ibid.*, p. 117.

8. *Ibid.*, p. 121.

9. *Ibid.*, p. 338.

10. *Ibid.*

Chapter 9   Morality

1. Piaget, *The Moral Judgment of the Child*, p. 55–56.

2. *Ibid.*, p. 66.

3. *Ibid.*, p. 111.
4. *Ibid.*, p. 180.
5. *Ibid.*, p. 133.
6. *Ibid.*, p. 144.
7. *Ibid.*, p. 191.
8. *Ibid.*, p. 198.
9. *Ibid.*
10. *Ibid.*, p. 201.
11. *Ibid.*, p. 213.
12. *Ibid.*, p. 256.
13. *Ibid.*, p. 261.
14. *Ibid.*, pp. 319–320.

Chapter 10   Emotional Development

1. Piaget, *The Psychology of Intelligence*, p. 6.
2. Piaget, *Play, Dreams, and Imitation in Childhood*, p. 207.
3. Piaget, *Six Psychological Studies*, Chap. I.
4. Inhelder and Piaget, *The Growth of Logical Thinking from Childhood to Adolescence*, p. 349.
5. Piaget, *Six Psychological Studies*, p. 36.
6. *Ibid.*, pp. 54–55.
7. *Ibid.*, p. 59.
8. Inhelder and Piaget, *The Growth of Logical Thinking from Childhood to Adolescence*, p. 349.
9. Piaget, *Six Psychological Studies*, p. 69.
10. *Ibid.*, pp. 68–69.

Chapter 11   Play and Imitation

1. Piaget, *Play, Dreams, and Imitation in Childhood*, p. 87.
2. *Ibid.*
3. *Ibid.*, p. 92.
4. *Ibid.*, p. 10.
5. *Ibid.*, p. 51.
6. *Ibid.*, p. 63.
7. *Ibid.*, p. 93.
8. *Ibid.*, p. 94.
9. *Ibid.*, p. 97.
10. *Ibid.*, p. 125.
11. *Ibid.*, p. 121.

12. *Ibid.*, p. 131.
13. *Ibid.*, p. 132.
14. *Ibid.*, pp. 133–134.
15. *Ibid.*, p. 134.
16. *Ibid.*, p. 136.
17. *Ibid.*, p. 138.
18. *Ibid.*, p. 139.
19. *Ibid.*, p. 141.
20. *Ibid.*, p. 142.
21. *Ibid.*
22. *Ibid.*, p. 154.
23. *Ibid.*, p. 166.
24. *Ibid.*, p. 168.
25. *Ibid.*, p. 289.
26. See Jerome L. Singer, *Daydreaming: An Introduction to the Experimental Study of Inner Experience.*
27. J. Nina Lieberman, "Playfulness: An Attempt to Conceptualize a Quality of Play and the Player," *Psychological Reports*, 19 (1966), 278.
28. David P. Weikart, *The Cognitively Oriented Curriculum, A Framework for Preschool Teachers* (in press). Described in *Education Daily*, Dec. 1, 1970, pp. 4–6.
29. Mary Ann S. Pulaski, "Play as a Function of Toy Structure and Fantasy Predisposition," *Child Development*, 41 (1970), 531–537.

Chapter 12   Representation

1. Piaget, *Play, Dreams, and Imitation in Childhood*, p. 216.
2. *Ibid.*, pp. 225–226.
3. *Ibid.*, p. 231.
4. *Ibid.*, pp. 229–230.
5. *Ibid.*, p. 270.
6. *Ibid.*, p. 287.
7. *Ibid.*, pp. 289–290.

Chapter 13   Numbers

1. L. G. Marsh, *Approach to Mathematics*, p. 19.
2. Quoted in *ibid.*

3. See Catherine Stern and Margaret B. Stern, *Children Discover Arithmetic*, rev. ed. (New York: Harper & Row, 1971).
4. Piaget, *Six Psychological Studies*, p. 53.
5. Piaget, *The Child's Conception of Number*, p. 47.
6. *Ibid.*, p. 64.
7. *Ibid.*, pp. 124–125.
8. *Ibid.*, p. 127.
9. *Ibid.*, p. 134.
10. *Ibid.*, p. 149.
11. *Ibid.*, p. 167.
12. *Ibid.*, p. 187.
13. *Ibid.*, p. 189.

Chapter 14   The Geometry of Space

1. Piaget, "How Children Form Mathematical Concepts," in R. C. Anderson and D. P. Ausubel (eds.), *Readings in the Psychology of Cognition*, p. 409.
2. *Ibid.*, p. 410.
3. See Piaget, Inhelder, and Szeminska, *The Child's Conception of Geometry*, Chap. 3.
4. Piaget, "How Children Form Mathematical Concepts," p. 412.
5. Piaget, Inhelder, and Szeminska, *The Child's Conception of Geometry*, p. 34.
6. Piaget, "How Children Form Mathematical Concepts," p. 412.
7. Piaget, Inhelder, and Szeminska, *The Child's Conception of Geometry*, pp. 45–46.
8. *Ibid.*, pp. 52–53.
9. *Ibid.*, p. 168.
10. *Ibid.*, p. 263.

Chapter 15   Perception and Learning

1. A. Ames, Jr., "Visual Perception and the Rotating Trapezoidal Window," *Psychological Monographs*, 65, No. 7 (1951).
2. Piaget, *The Mechanisms of Perception*, p. 84.
3. *Ibid.*, p. 71.
4. *Ibid.*
5. Flavell, *The Developmental Psychology of Jean Piaget*, p. 231.
6. Piaget, *The Mechanisms of Perception*, pp. 315 ff.

7. Piaget, Inhelder, and Szeminska, *The Child's Conception of Geometry*, pp. 95 ff.
8. Piaget, *The Mechanisms of Perception*, p. 359.
9. For reviews, see Eleanor Gibson and Vivian Olum, "Experimental Methods of Studying Perception in Children," in P. Mussen (ed.), *Handbook of Research Methods in Child Development*; and Joachim Wohlwill, "Developmental Studies of Perception," *Psychological Bulletin*, 57 (1960), 249–288.
10. Gloria Wolinsky, "Piaget's Theory of Perception," in *Training School Bulletin*, 62 (1965), 20.
11. Piaget and Inhelder, *The Psychology of the Child*, p. 32.
12. J. McV. Hunt, *Intelligence and Experience*.
13. I. Sigel and F. H. Hooper (eds.), *Logical Thinking in Children*, p. 424.

Chapter 16   Time

1. Piaget, *The Construction of Reality in the Child*, p. 320.
2. *Ibid.*, p. 335.
3. *Ibid.*, pp. 346–347.
4. Piaget, *The Child's Conception of Time*, p. 202.
5. *Ibid.*, p. 204.
6. *Ibid.*, p. 209.
7. *Ibid.*, p. 210.
8. *Ibid.*, p. 223.
9. *Ibid.*, p. 224.
10. *Ibid.*, p. 234.
11. *Ibid.*, p. 240.
12. *Ibid.*, p. 13.
13. *Ibid.*, p. 16.
14. *Ibid.*, pp. 26–27.
15. *Ibid.*, pp. 64–65.
16. *Ibid.*, pp. 179–180.

Chapter 17   Movement and Speed

1. Piaget, *The Child's Conception of Movement and Speed*, p. 6.
2. *Ibid.*, p. 7.
3. *Ibid.*, pp. 16–17.
4. *Ibid.*, p. 24.

5. *Ibid.*, p. 28.
6. *Ibid.*, p. 123.
7. *Ibid.*, p. 61.
8. *Ibid.*, p. 163.
9. *Ibid.*, pp. 157–158.

Chapter 18 Education

1. Piaget, *Science of Education and the Psychology of the Child,*
   p. 7.
2. *Ibid.*, p. 8.
3. *Ibid.*
4. *Ibid.*, pp. 11–12.
5. *Ibid.*, p. 13.
6. *Ibid.*, p. 14.
7. *Ibid.*, p. 17.
8. *Ibid.*
9. *Ibid.*, pp. 28–29.
10. *Ibid.*, p. 51.
11. *Ibid.*, p. 36.
12. Ripple and Rockcastle, *Piaget Rediscovered*, p. 40.
13. Piaget, *Science of Education and the Psychology of the Child,*
    p. 130.
14. *Ibid.*, p. 132.
15. Ripple and Rockcastle, *Piaget Rediscovered*, p. 5.
16. From a speech given at the 1969 Conference of the National
    Association of Independent Schools, at which the author
    moderated a panel on "Individualizing the Elementary Class-
    room."
17. For more about the British schools, see the fine series of
    articles by Joseph Featherstone in *The New Republic*, Aug.
    19, Sept. 2, and Sept. 9, 1967. Reprints are available from
    The New Republic, 1244 19th Street, N.W., Washington, D.C.
    20036. See also "An English Lesson for America" by the same
    author, in *The New York Times Book Review*, Sept. 20, 1970,
    pp. 10 ff. More and more American schools are beginning to
    move toward a less rigid, more informal classroom. See the
    description of North Dakota schools in *The New York Times*,
    Oct. 11, 1970, p. 68.

18. Piaget, *Science of Education and the Psychology of the Child*, p. 27.

19. *Ibid.*, p. 69.

20. *Ibid.*

21. *Ibid.*, p. 77.

22. *Ibid.*, p. 108.

23. *Ibid.*

24. Neil Postman and Charles Weingartner, *Teaching as a Subversive Activity*.

25. Piaget, *Science of Education and the Psychology of the Child*, p. 124.

26. *Ibid.*

glossary

ACCOMMODATION. *See* Adaptation.

ADAPTATION. A biological mode of functioning which characterizes all forms and levels of life. It consists of the dual processes of assimilation and accommodation, which go on continuously. *Assimilation* is the process of taking in from the environment all forms of stimulation and information, which are then digested and reintegrated into the organism's existing forms or structures. *Accommodation* is the process of reaching out and adjusting to new and changing conditions in the environment, so that pre-existing patterns of behavior are modified to cope with new information or situations.

AFFECT. The emotional aspect of behavior which includes feelings, motivation, interest, and values.

ANIMISM. The child's belief that everything in nature is endowed with life and purpose, like himself (e.g., the sun follows to watch over him, the wind blows to keep him cool).

ARTIFICIALISM. The child's belief that human beings created natural phenomena such as the sun, the moon, lakes, rivers, and mountains.

ASSIMILATION. *See* Adaptation.

CENTRATION. The first, immediate aspect of perception, which involves *centering* or focusing upon the most compelling features of that which is perceived, to the exclusion of other aspects. (*See* Decentration.)

CIRCULAR REACTION. The repetition of a sensory-motor pattern of response until it becomes strengthened and consolidated into a new schema. Later, it may be repeated with variations in order to produce varied effects.

COGNITION. Refers to all the intellective activities of the mind, such as thinking, knowing, remembering, perceiving, recognizing, or generalizing.

COGNITIVE CONFLICT. A period of stress or disequilibrium caused by the assimilation of new information which is not in harmony with previous knowledge. This forces the child to accommodate on a higher level of thinking, in order to incorporate the new information and restore mental equilibrium. (*See* Equilibration.)

COLLECTIVE MONOLOGUE. The egocentric conversations of preoperational children who talk to each other but pay little attention to what the other child is saying and pursue their own lines of thought.

COLLECTIVE SYMBOLISM. Play in which children take different roles and act them out with full awareness of each other and of their separate roles.

COMPENSATORY PLAY. The child's "make-believe" play in which he acts out fear, anger, and other emotions in gradual degrees so that he can cope with them (e.g., playing hospital for children who face a feared operation).

CONCRETE OPERATIONS. *See* Operations.

CONSERVATION. The ability to understand that objects or quantities are "conserved" and remain constant despite changes in their appearance (e.g., one cup of milk is the same amount whether poured into a tall, thin glass or a wide, shallow bowl).

DECENTRATION. The secondary and continuing aspect of perceptual activity, by means of which errors or distortions of perception are corrected. Perception focuses first upon the most compelling aspect of a stimulus to the exclusion of others; decentration, or focusing on secondary aspects and incorporating them into the total percept, leads to modified and more accurate perception.

DEFERRED IMITATION. *See* Imitation.

DIRECTED GROPING. The experimental variation of a familiar behavior pattern in order to observe what will happen. This occurs during the second year of sensory-motor development.

EGOCENTRISM. Lack of awareness of anything outside the realm of one's immediate experience. It is evidenced most clearly in infants, who are unaware even of their own hands and feet as being parts of their bodies and do not realize that objects exist when they can no longer be seen. Egocentric thinking persists throughout childhood, as shown by the child's unawareness of points of view other than his own, and his projection of his own wishes, fears, and desires onto the world around him.

ELEMENTARY ERRORS. Errors of perception which lead to overestimation of stimuli under certain conditions.

EQUILIBRATION. The process of regulating assimilation and accommodation in order to maintain a state of internal balance or *equilibrium*. This protects the organism from being overwhelmed with new and incomprehensible information which it has not assimilated and also from overreaching itself in the attempt to accommodate to a too rapidly changing environment. (*See* Adaptation.)

EXPERIENCE. Used by Piaget to refer to the physical and empirical experiences of children which contribute to their knowledge of the world through their senses and their muscles.

FORMAL OPERATIONS. *See* Operations.

GENETIC EPISTEMOLOGY. The developmental study of the nature of knowledge; how it begins and how it develops.

GROUPINGS. Organized structures of thought which are reversible and logical in the sense that every element is related to every other element. They include the logic of classes and relations and are characteristic of the period of concrete operations.

HYPOTHETICO-DEDUCTIVE THINKING. Inferential thinking which follows a hypothesis through to all possible logical conclusions. It is based on theory rather than fact, and is characteristic of the period of formal operations.

IMITATION. Represents the child's attempt to adjust to the environment. It is based primarily upon the accommodation of the child to what he observes around him, whether he understands (i.e., has assimilated) it or not. *Deferred imitation*—imitation of something observed in the past, which indicates the child's emerging ability to remember.

INNATE OR NEONATAL REFLEXES. Behavior patterns which are present at birth, such as sucking and grasping.

INRC GROUPS. Logico-mathematical groups characterized by four kinds of transformations: *I*dentity, *N*egation, *R*eciprocity, and *C*orrelation. They occur in the thinking of the period of formal operations.

INTERIORIZATION. The gradual dissociation between external actions and the mental representations which replace them (e.g., the action of counting aloud while touching each of five blocks becomes interiorized as a numerical concept of the number five).

INTUITIVE REASONING. Characteristic of the preoperational child between four and seven. It is based on immediate perception but through trial and error may lead to correct conclusions.

LUDIC SYMBOLISM. The playful symbolism of children's "make-believe" games in which objects are used to represent other objects not present (e.g., a stick is used as a gun, or a rag doll becomes a baby).

MATURATION. The emergence of patterns of development which are innate within the organism and appear in sequential order in all normal development.

MORAL REALISM. The young child's view that the severity of punishment should depend on the amount of damage done, regardless of intention (e.g., it is worse to break six glasses accidentally than one glass deliberately because six glasses cost more than one).

MORALITY OF CONSTRAINT. Based on a sense of moral realism. Punishment is meted out according to the amount of damage done, regardless of intention. The harshest punishment is the fairest. Characteristic of preoperational children.

MORALITY OF COOPERATION. Takes into account the motives and degree of responsibility of the offending child. Punishment is not based just on the amount of damage done. Characteristic of the period of concrete operations.

OBJECT CONSTANCY. An intellectual achievement of the sensory-motor period in which the baby learns that objects and people exist independently of his perception of them.

OPERATIONS. The interiorized activities of the mind, as opposed to the sensory-motor or physical activities of the body. Characterized by logical thought processes which are reversible. *Concrete operations* are concerned with concrete, existing objects and include ordering, serial arrangements, and classification, as well as mathematical processes. *Formal or Second-order operations* are concerned with logical propositions and hypothetical reasoning, based on theoretical constructs rather than concrete objects.

PERCEPTION. The direct and immediate first impression of objects or situations perceived. (*See* Centration.)

PERCEPTUAL ACTIVITY. The continuing aspect of perception which modifies and corrects the often inaccurate first perception by focusing on other aspects of the stimulus and incorporating all perceptions into a more accurate whole. (*See* Decentration.)

PERCEPTUAL CONSTANCY. The ability to perceive objects as constant in size, shape, color, etc., even when seen in changing settings which make them appear different (e.g., a man is perceived as life-sized even when seen from a block away so that he actually appears much smaller).

PERCEPTUAL REASONING. Based on immediate appearances. Characteristic of the preoperational child who focuses on only one aspect of a stimulus at a time. (*See* Intuitive reasoning.)

PRECONCEPTS. The child's first, fuzzy attempts at generalization, in which he confuses representatives of a class with the whole class. Preconceptual thinking characterizes the child between two and four years old.

PREOPERATIONAL. Refers to the period of early childhood preceding the emergence of logical, reversible operations. Characterized by egocentric thinking and illogical intuitions based upon perception.

REALISM. The child's belief that whatever is real to him, such as dreams, feelings, or pictures, has objective reality and is shared by other people.

REPRESENTATION. The process by which an image, a sign, or a symbol comes to represent an external reality. In symbolic play, a child may use acorns to represent nonexistent dishes. Memories are interiorized images, whereas words are verbal signs which represent complexes of socially shared meanings.

REVERSIBILITY. A characteristic of logical operations which permits the mind to reverse its activity and go backward in thought in order to coordinate previously observed phenomena with present circumstances (e.g., if 2 and 2 make 4, then 4 less 2 leaves 2 once more).

SCHEMA (plural, SCHEMAS or SCHEMATA). A mental structure or pattern of behavior arising out of the integration of simpler, more primitive units into an enlarged and more complex whole (e.g., many separate finger movements gradually become coordinated into the complex skill of piano playing).

SENSORY-MOTOR. Refers to learning based on information received through physical exploration and sensory stimulation.

SOCIAL TRANSMISSION. A form of learning which depends on verbal instruction and experiences of a social or cultural nature.

STAGES. Levels of development characterized by successively more complex and more highly integrated patterns of thought or behavior. Usually characteristic of certain chronological ages.

SYMBOLIC PLAY. The child's "make-believe" fantasies in which assimilation predominates, as the child uses objects to represent in his play other objects which are not present, but which he is seeking to understand or familiarize himself with (e.g., the child uses leaves and twigs to represent papers and pencils as he "plays school").

SYMBOLIC REPRESENTATION. Refers to objects which are used to represent other objects as in Symbolic Play (above). (*See also* Representation.)

TOPOLOGY. The study of spatial relationships and forms without size or shape. Deals with open and closed figures such as a simple closed curve which divides a plane into inside and outside.

works cited in text

Ames, A., Jr. "Visual Perception and the Rotating Trapezoidal Window." *Psychological Monographs*, 65, No. 7 (1951).

Baldwin, Alfred L. *Theories of Child Development*. New York: Wiley & Sons, 1968.

Bruner, Jerome S. *The Process of Education*. New York: Vintage Books, 1960.

Bruner, Jerome S., Olver, Rose, and Greenfield, Patricia, et al. *Studies in Cognitive Growth*. New York: Wiley & Sons, 1966.

Dennis, Wayne. "Piaget's Questions Applied to a Child of Known Environment." *Journal of Genetic Psychology*, 60 (1942), 307–320.

Elkind, David. *Children and Adolescents: Interpretive Essays on Jean Piaget*. New York: Oxford University Press, 1970.

Flavell, John H. *The Developmental Psychology of Jean Piaget*. Princeton, N.J.: D. Van Nostrand Co., 1963.

Gibson, Eleanor, and Olum, Vivian. "Experimental Methods of Studying Perception in Children." In Paul Mussen (ed.), *Hand-*

book of Research Methods in Child Development. New York: John Wiley & Sons, 1960, pp. 311–373.

Hunt, J. McV. Intelligence and Experience. New York: Ronald, 1961.

Inhelder, Bärbel, and Piaget, Jean. The Early Growth of Logic in the Child. New York: Norton, 1969.

———. The Growth of Logical Thinking from Childhood to Adolescence. New York: Basic Books, 1958.

Lieberman, J. Nina. "Playfulness: An Attempt to Conceptualize a Quality of Play and the Player." Psychological Reports, 19 (1966), 278.

Maier, Henry W. Three Theories of Child Development. New York: Harper & Row, 1965.

Marsh, L. G. Approach to Mathematics. London: A. & C. Black Ltd., 1969.

Piaget, Jean. "Autobiography." In E. G. Boring, et al., History of Psychology in Autobiography, Vol. 4. Worcester, Mass.: Clark University Press, 1952, pp. 237–256.

———. "The Child and Modern Physics." Scientific American, 196, 3 (1957), 46–51.

———. "Children's Philosophies." In C. Murchison (ed.), Handbook of Child Psychology, 2d ed. Worcester, Mass.: Clark University Press, 1933, pp. 534–547.

———. The Child's Conception of Movement and Speed. New York: Basic Books, 1970.

———. The Child's Conception of Number. New York: Norton, 1965.

———. The Child's Conception of Physical Causality. Totowa, N.J.: Littlefield, Adams & Co., 1960.

———. The Child's Conception of the World. Totowa, N.J.: Littlefield, Adams & Co., 1965.

———. The Child's Conception of Time. New York: Basic Books, 1970.

———. The Construction of Reality in the Child. New York: Basic Books, 1954.

———. "The Definition of Stages of Development." In J. M. Tanner and B. Inhelder (eds.), Discussions on Child Development, Vol. IV. New York: International Universities Press, 1960, pp. 116–135.

———. "Development and Learning." In Richard E. Ripple and Verne N. Rockcastle (eds.), *Piaget Rediscovered: A Report of the Conference on Cognitive Studies and Curriculum Development,* March, 1964. Ithaca, N.Y.: School of Education, Cornell University.

———. "The Development of Time Concepts in the Child." In P. H. Hoch and J. Zubin (eds.), *Psychopathology of Childhood.* New York: Grune & Stratton, 1955, pp. 34–44.

———. *Genetic Epistemology.* New York: Columbia University Press, 1970.

———. "How Children Form Mathematical Concepts." In R. C. Anderson and D. P. Ausubel (eds.), *Readings in the Psychology of Cognition.* New York: Holt, Rinehart and Winston, 1965, pp. 406–414.

———. *Judgment and Reasoning in the Child.* Totowa, N.J.: Littlefield, Adams & Co., 1959.

———. *The Language and Thought of the Child.* Cleveland, Ohio: World Publishing Co., 1955.

———. *Logic and Psychology.* New York: Basic Books, 1957. (Out of print.)

———. *The Mechanisms of Perception.* New York: Basic Books, 1969.

———. *The Moral Judgment of the Child.* New York: Free Press, 1965.

———. *The Origins of Intelligence in Children.* New York: Norton, 1963.

———. "Peering into the Mind of a Child." *The UNESCO Courier,* 12 (1959), 4–7.

———. "Perceptual and Cognitive (or Operational) Structures in the Development of the Concept of Space in the Child." *Proceedings of the 14th International Congress of Psychologists* (1954), pp. 41–46.

———. "Piaget's Theory." In P. Mussen (ed.), *Carmichael's Manual of Child Psychology,* Vol. I, 3d ed. New York: Wiley, 1970, pp. 703–732.

———. *Play, Dreams, and Imitation in Childhood.* New York: Norton, 1962.

———. "Principal Factors Determining Intellectual Evolution from Childhood to Adult Life." In E. L. Hartley and R. E. Hartley (eds.), *Outside Readings in Psychology*, 2d ed. New York: Crowell, 1958, pp. 43–55.

———. "The Problem of Consciousness and Symbolic Processes." In H. E. Abramson (ed.), *Problems of Consciousness: Transactions of the Fourth Conference*, March 24–31, Princeton, N.J. New York: Josiah Macy Foundation, 1954.

———. *The Psychology of Intelligence*. Paterson, N.J.: Littlefield, Adams & Co., 1960.

———. "The Right to Education in the Modern World." In UNESCO, *Freedom and Culture*. New York: Columbia University Press, 1951, pp. 67–116.

———. *Science of Education and the Psychology of the Child*. New York: Orion Press, 1970.

———. *Six Psychological Studies*. New York: Random House, 1967.

———. *Structuralism*. New York: Basic Books, 1970.

———. "Understanding and Verbal Explanation Between Young Children of the Same Age." In G. E. Swanson, T. M. Newcomb, and E. L. Hartley (eds.), *Readings in Social Psychology*. New York: Holt, 1952, pp. 54–66.

Piaget, Jean, and Inhelder, Bärbel. *The Child's Conception of Space*. New York: Norton, 1967.

———. *The Psychology of the Child*. New York: Basic Books, 1969.

Piaget, Jean, Inhelder, Bärbel, and Szeminska, Alina. *The Child's Conception of Geometry*. New York: Basic Books, 1960.

Piaget, Jean, Inhelder, Bärbel, et al. *Mental Imagery in the Child*. New York: Basic Books, 1971.

Piaget, Jean, and Weil, A. "The Development in Children of the Idea of the Homeland and of Relations with Other Countries." *International Social Sciences Bulletin*, 3 (1951), 561–578.

Postman, Neil, and Weingartner, Charles. *Teaching as a Subversive Activity*. New York: Delacorte Press, 1969.

Pulaski, Mary Ann S. "Play as a Function of Toy Structure and Fantasy Predisposition." *Child Development*, 41 (1970), 531–537.

Ripple, Richard E., and Rockcastle, Verne O. (eds.). *Piaget Rediscovered: A Report of the Conference on Cognitive Studies and Curriculum Development*, March, 1964. Ithaca, N.Y., School of Education, Cornell University.

Russell, Roger W., and Dennis, Wayne. "Studies in Animism: I. A Standardized Procedure for the Investigation of Animism." *Journal of Genetic Psychology*, 55 (1939), 389–400.

Sigel, Irving E., and Hooper, Frank H. (eds.). *Logical Thinking in Children: Research Based on Piaget's Theory.* New York: Holt, Rinehart and Winston, 1968.

Singer, Jerome L. *Daydreaming: An Introduction to the Experimental Study of Inner Experience.* New York: Random House, 1966.

Smedslund, Jan, "The Acquisition of Conservation of Substance and Weight in Children." In Irving E. Sigel and Frank H. Hooper (eds.), *Logical Thinking in Children.* New York: Holt, Rinehart and Winston, 1968, pp. 265–295.

Stern, Catherine, and Stern, Margaret B., *Children Discover Arithmetic*, rev. ed. New York: Harper & Row, 1971.

Wohlwill, Joachim. "Developmental Studies of Perception." *Psychological Bulletin*, 57 (1960), 249–288.

Wolinsky, Gloria. "Piaget's Theory of Perception: Insights for Educational Practices with Children Who Have Perceptual Difficulty." *Training School Bulletin*, 62 (May, 1965), 12–25.